Family Business Succession

Family Business Publications are the combined efforts of the Family Business Consulting Group and Palgrave Macmillan. These books provide useful information on a broad range of topics that concern the family business enterprise, including succession planning, communication, strategy and growth, family leadership, and more. The books are written by experts with combined experiences of over a century in the field of family enterprise and who have consulted with thousands of enterprising families the world over, giving the reader practical, effective, and time-tested insights to everyone involved in a family business.

FBG, founded in 1994, is the leading business consultancy exclusively devoted to helping family enterprises prosper across generations.

Family Business Succession

Your Roadmap to Continuity

Kelly LeCouvie and
Jennifer Pendergast

FAMILY BUSINESS SUCCESSION

First published in 2014 by
PALGRAVE MACMILLAN®
in the United States—a division of St. Martin's Press LLC,
175 Fifth Avenue, New York, NY 10010.

Where this book is distributed in the UK, Europe and the rest of the world,
this is by Palgrave Macmillan, a division of Macmillan Publishers Limited,
registered in England, company number 785998, of Houndmills,
Basingstoke, Hampshire RG21 6XS.

Palgrave Macmillan is the global academic imprint of the above companies
and has companies and representatives throughout the world.

Palgrave® and Macmillan® are registered trademarks in the United States,
the United Kingdom, Europe and other countries.

ISBN: 978–1–137–28089–3

Library of Congress Cataloging-in-Publication Data

LeCouvie, Kelly.
    Family business succession : your roadmap to continuity / Kelly LeCouvie
and Jennifer Pendergast.
        pages cm.—(A Family business publication)
    ISBN 978–1–137–28089–3 (alk. paper)
        1. Family-owned business enterprises—Management. 2. Family-owned
business enterprises—Succession. I. Pendergast, Jennifer M. II. Title.

HD62.25.L433 2014
658.1′6—dc23   2013027595

A catalogue record of the book is available from the British Library.

Design by Newgen Knowledge Works (P) Ltd., Chennai, India.

First edition: January 2014

10 9 8 7 6 5 4 3 2 1

Printed in the United States of America.

For my family, who by example give me reasons every day to applaud family businesses

—Kelly LeCouvie

To my family whose support and encouragement allow me to reach other families

—Jennifer Pendergast

Contents

Acknowledgments

We are both grateful for our colleagues at FBCG who provide great experiential insights on family business continuity; we were inspired by their work and their wisdom in writing this book. We would also like to thank Jeff Wuorio for his help in bringing this book to fruition—he challenged and helped clarify our thinking. Finally, we thank our clients and our teachers, who have so generously shared their experiences.

I

The Opportunities and Challenges of Continuity

Family businesses often outperform nonfamily businesses. This is true for a number of reasons. One of the primary sources of success for business-owning families is their focus on ensuring continuity of both the business and the family. Longevity is typically foremost in the minds of family business owners, and, unlike many of their competitors in nonfamily businesses, they think about long-term viability and continued family engagement. This is a testament not only to their focus on the future of the business but to the faith family shareholders hold in each other and in their ability to navigate the challenges that also come with working with family members.

If you are reading this book, it is likely that you are associated in some way with a family business, either as a family or nonfamily member. And you may have possibly experienced that increased complexity that comes with growth in the family through generations. From evaluating a family member's job performance to deciding whether spouses will be invited to work in the business or selecting family members to serve on the board, seemingly every decision has to be made with the family as an important consideration.

The impact of family dynamics on business decision-making is often most apparent at the time of a generational transition. Many opportunities emerge for business-owning families in their pursuit of generational transitions. They learn more about their collective vision for the future; communication typically increases; family members get the chance to share their perceptions of the legacy, the business and the family's future; and the family typically bonds in ways that are distinct from other efforts.

There are also numerous challenges associated with planning for business and ownership continuity. The delicate questions of who ascends to what leadership role, who is invited to be an owner, and who holds whom accountable, can either strengthen the business and the family or wreak utter havoc with both.

The Jimenez Furniture Company was started by Mark and Andy Jimenez. Like any start-up, they encountered a host of challenges, including establishing a customer base, building production capacity, and raising necessary capital. Despite many hurdles, what worked to their advantage was the simplicity of their financial arrangement. The brothers owned the business in an even 50–50 split. In addition, each gave the other the latitude to make decisions in his area of expertise, Mark in production and Andy in sales. As a result, they rarely disagreed. When they did, they resolved issues by relying on the respect and trust they had developed over the years of growing up together.

Unfortunately, this arrangement couldn't withstand the test of time. As the business grew, Mark's two sons joined as salespeople. Of Andy's three children, only his daughter opted to join the company. While not quite so elementary as a 50–50 division of ownership, it was still a fairly straightforward arrangement when Mark and Andy decided to retire and pass the business along to their children. Mark elected to retain 10 percent and give 20 percent to each of his sons, who had joined the business (an easy decision since he didn't have any other children). His thinking was to retain some involvement in decision-making, while at the same time providing room for the next generation. Andy also retained 10 percent. He decided to divide his remaining 40 percent by giving 20 percent to his daughter, who was in the business, and 10 percent to each of his sons, who worked elsewhere.

All of these decisions reflected the two brothers' desire to maintain equality of ownership for those involved in the business and give them control over decision-making while allowing nonemployed children to benefit from the business as well.

By the third generation, things became much more complicated. Some third-generation children joined the business, but they represented a minority of the owners. A few spouses sought jobs at the business as well, some well qualified and others not quite so experienced. In addition, other individuals from outside the family had established themselves as valuable executives worthy of leadership positions. And, as the family continued to grow, the business strained to provide sufficient financial rewards for everyone with a share in the company, including family members with an ownership stake who had not worked in the business.

Looking back, Mark and Andy were astonished that their once straightforward furniture business had become so complicated. Family members began to squabble as to which of them was best qualified to move up into leadership positions once the second generation of owners stepped down. While other family members displayed little interest in actually participating in the business, they had expectations of a healthy cash distribution every year. Facing what they deemed to be an unsolvable situation, the Jimenez family decided to sell the business to a competitor.

While the Jimenez brothers demonstrated success at building a business, they overlooked one absolutely critical step—careful planning and analysis of business continuity through future generations. As a result, implicit expectations were never discussed, including the desire to retain the family within the business; a philosophy concerning how to balance family and business interests; and expectations of how the business should be managed. Had Mark and Andy taken the time to include the second- and third generations in these conversations and ensure both generations understood what it would take to achieve those expectations, they might have been successful in mapping out a generational transition for both leadership and ownership.

Any number of factors can contribute to the breakdown of family businesses. But no matter the causes, the Jimenez story illustrates the enormous importance of family business continuity planning. Absent dedicated effort to continuity planning, even the most prosperous family business may struggle to create a strong foundation for effective leadership and ownership transitions through generations.

Before we move on to examine what we will cover in this book, it will be helpful to take a closer look at some terminology. Although "succession planning" is the term many use to describe the strategies and processes to pass leadership and ownership from one generation of owners to the next, we find it useful to define the process in terms of continuity. Succession connotes an event, something with a defined beginning and end. Continuity, on the other hand, suggests an ongoing process.

This distinction is important because succession planning is really a lifelong process, one that merits the ongoing attention of multiple business stakeholders and one that should always be on the owning family's radar screen. It's just as critical to recognize that the process is never really complete. As we will demonstrate, ensuring continuity requires careful thought and planning, a great deal of discussion, inclusion of family members as well as nonfamily management and the board of directors, and an ongoing focus on what the family wants for the future of the business and themselves.

That makes continuity planning a mindset, a part of the family and business culture and an ongoing effort with essentially no conclusion. The focus is not solely on passing the business from one generation to the next, but establishing a clear rationale and purpose for continuity of the business, one that supports the family's mission, values, and goals.

Continuity planning requires proactive effort. By the time a son or daughter is in a leadership role, they likely have grown children who, in turn, are thinking about their future in the business. Continuity planning requires consistent attention so that progress is smooth and systematic.

As we describe in more detail later in the book, that attention should permeate almost every action and decision. For instance, when making a new management hire, it's helpful to consider how that individual might be included in the business' plan for continuity. Proactive business leaders will make key decisions—new hires, diversification initiatives, and geographic expansion, for example—with business continuity as a backdrop for those choices. They will ask themselves whether key strategic moves will be supported by the necessary infrastructure to steward the company through the next generation. Similarly, owners will make decisions in light of their desire for continuity, including their expectations for liquidity, and the rules and process for passing stock to succeeding generations.

The Middleton family owns a large international business that manufactures baby clothes. They have plants in the United States, Mexico, and China, and plan to expand into India. Peter Middleton, the third-generation family CEO, works with two siblings and four cousins. In addition, there are 32 family shareholders who are not in the business. The Middleton family decided during the second-generation leadership period to form a family council as well as a professional board of directors to help ensure that family and business issues would be addressed in a proactive manner— before the "issues" became "problems." As a result of ongoing family meetings as well as meetings with advisers (which included estate planners, wealth management and family business consultants), the family feels included, informed, and comfortable with the circumstances under which leadership and ownership transitions will take place. They have developed their interpersonal skills, and believe that trust and respect have emerged over time, due to hard work on their part and a commitment to ongoing continuity plan.

While the example of the Jimenez family alludes to some of the challenges involved in achieving continuity, the Middleton family's efforts in continuity planning provide evidence that good outcomes can also be achieved by the family. As you might have experienced, increased complexity is associated with growth in the family. The greater the number of family members both inside and outside the business, the more complicated succession planning can become.

The evolutionary process of the business also complicates continuity. The first generation of ownership works extremely hard and typically reinvests their earnings in the business, although they may begin to accumulate wealth. While the second generation builds on that wealth and, in many cases, grows the business exponentially, the tipping point often comes with the third generation. This generation often enjoys financial means that were unavailable to the previous two generations, providing access to educational opportunities and, quite possibly, career choices other than the family business.

An emotional component is another factor. Not only may third-generation members pursue other professional options, but those who are interested in joining the business can become discouraged after listening to older family members complain about business and family challenges.

Still another element is the broader base of family members who enter the business. Cousins and in-laws may now play a prominent role in the business. Having been raised in different households, these family members may develop a different perspective on the business than others who grew up together. Sometimes the blend of perspectives meshes beautifully. Often, the opposite is true.

The business itself plays a role in the complexity. Typically, the business will become larger and more challenging to manage as time passes. Informal management practices must be replaced with more sophisticated processes and structure. Senior leaders must be willing to delegate authority, often to people who are not members of the ownership group. And, higher levels of skill and experience are required. Continuity planning must take into account the needs of the business as well as the family.

These factors underscore the importance of comprehensive planning. It's important to recognize that continuity is intricately woven into the fabric of the business as well as the family. It is also interwoven with the issues of ownership and leadership as well as family and business governance structures that support sound decision-making.

As long-time consultants with the Family Business Consulting Group, we work with business-owning families who struggle with the challenges inherent in effective continuity planning. One interesting observation that derives from our experience is the number of family-owned companies that, in effect, take continuity as a given. They assume and expect that all family members hope that the business will last for generations to come.

We believe, however, that the goal of continuity cannot be taken for granted. Achieving continuity is a constant but at the same time rewarding task, and one that requires a unified group of owners who are actively pursuing that goal. To that end, when we work with clients, one of the first things we ask is whether they want their business to continue into the next generation.

At first, many look at us with skepticism. But, once they think about the situation from a broader perspective and begin to understand the issues we just discussed, they become aware of the intricacies that continuity presents. Maybe there are a number of family members who don't care about the business at all. Perhaps there are others whose career choices take them in a completely different direction. And, among those family members who do wish to be involved in the business, there may be conflicting perspectives on the future direction of the company.

If the ownership group does wish to continue the business, it's imperative to identify a shared vision for the future. Do owners see a business with as many family members as possible working in it? Do they want to expand geographically or stay within their current footprint? How much risk are they willing to take to grow? How can they assure management accountability in the future?

While there can be literally hundreds of decisions and choices along the journey, this book incorporates six themes that, when considered together, provide practical advice on how to effectively manage continuity planning. In the order in which we will address them, they are:

- **Vision.** What do you want the business to look like in the future? What role do you want the family to play? What values and principles will guide the family and the business?
- **Ownership.** Who will be allowed to participate in ownership? How can ownership be transferred most effectively? What can be done to ensure future owners are prepared for this great responsibility?

- **Leadership**. What leadership attributes will be required to manage the business into the future? How might this profile change as the business evolves? Are there systems and processes to ensure that the next generation of leaders will be prepared?
- **Business governance**. What oversight structure and processes are needed to ensure business success? How will owners and others participate to create an effective board of directors?
- **Family governance**. What structure and processes are required for effective family decision-making? What decisions will the family oversee, and who will be allowed to participate?
- **A culture of continuity**. What role does culture play in helping to ensure continuity?

At the end of the book, we'll tie all these themes together and share some tools and processes to manage continuity planning.

An obvious concern for many business owners is earmarking sufficient time and energy to address succession and continuity. With all that owners and other involved in the business have to focus on, where is the time for adequate attention to succession supposed to come from?

Throughout this book, we will emphasize a number of strategies to address this very real concern. Every business owner—no matter the generation—knows how lonely it can be "at the top," but that doesn't have to be the case when it comes to continuity planning. It's important that owners reach out to others for their help, support, and input. The most effective planning process requires the involvement of strong management, an active and involved board of directors, the input of trusted advisers, and a supportive family so that all generations can work together to make decisions with comfort and confidence.

There are many reasons to include nonfamily participants in the planning process. Nonfamily employees will be directly affected by any succession-related decisions. Involving senior leaders in the process engenders loyalty and gives them confidence that the business will continue to be successful in the future.

Beyond management, advisers to the family can provide an alternative perspective and depth to the continuity planning process. Because they are not part of the family or the business, they may see critical issues and challenges in a different light. Moreover, they may prove more objective and forthright, offering candid observations and feedback that some family members may be too intimidated to share.

It is important to recognize that continuity planning goes beyond who will eventually lead the business. Successful continuity depends on many initiatives managed by a diverse group, as well as an overall comfort level with change. For instance, the founder might develop a strategy for the business that is quite insular, but is one that works for her. However, a second- or third-generation member may not be able to adopt the same approach when the business is three times larger (and may not want to, regardless). We often hear next-generation members say they feel overwhelmed at the thought of managing the business the way Mom or Dad did. It has simply become too intimidating and too complex.

The failure to develop and carry out a comprehensive continuity plan can create significant complexity and anxiety for the next generation of leaders and owners. In contrast, a continuity plan that has been developed with appropriate participation and rigor will foster comfort, commitment, and confidence among the next generation and help equip them with the capabilities they require to successfully steward the business into the future. As we will discuss later, the most successful families are those that have built a culture of continuity, constantly focusing on what it will take to ensure the legacy of the family enterprise is perpetuated.

When business owners are asked what keeps them up at night, they often identify a concern about the future of their business. Understandably, they feel responsible for protecting the family's wealth and ensuring the transition of a healthy business to future generations.

Continuity planning can alleviate these worries. It helps ensure the continued success of the family business and the ability of those who follow to steward that success in alignment with the company's values and vision. Just as important, succession planning can be very liberating for those doing the planning. By putting into place policies, procedures, and strategies that bolster continuity, sleepless nights become more restful.

Continuity planning is a process that provides great insights for the family as well as an opportunity for them to plan for the future as a collective. It can force those involved to make some tough, occasionally uncomfortable, decisions. Yet those decisions often yield unforeseen benefits: a more bonded family, a stronger business, and a culture of unity and trust. Consider this book both a valued guide and companion as you make your way through the critical process of succession and continuity planning.

In Brief

- Continuity planning and execution should be proactive.
- Continuity planning can foster confidence among senior-generation family members in the long-term stability of the business.
- Effective continuity planning can encourage a culture of inclusion as various family members take part in the process.
- The process of continuity planning helps participants build valuable interpersonal skills.
- Nonfamily members provide valuable alternative perspectives to the continuity planning process.
- Continuity planning is an ongoing process that contributes to the health of the family and the business.

2

The Foundation of Continuity:
A Vision for the Future

The journey you are about to take in continuity planning can be exciting, fun, and challenging at the same time. Some families inadvertently make continuity planning more difficult than it needs to be by skipping or rushing through fundamental questions that we encourage you to think very carefully about. For example, does the family want to continue the business into the next generation? If so, in what ways might ownership of the business evolve? What do they want the business to achieve? Can they perpetuate the business with nonfamily leaders?

These and other pivotal questions form the foundation for a shared vision of the future to effectively steward a generational transition. A vision provides affirmation that the family wants to continue the business into the next generation and addresses critical questions that every business-owning family should consider in terms of who they are and where they wish the business to go.

In this chapter, we will discuss the importance of shared values and a vision for the future, as well as a decision-making process to put these important components into place. We will also provide sample vision statements from other families and share methodologies for creating a vision.

Vision Defined

The term "vision" has different meanings for different people. While many are acquainted with business vision statements, a family vision may be less familiar.

In one sense, vision can be boiled down to identifying what the family sees as its ideal future. They may ask, what as a family do we most desire as an ultimate outcome for the business and for ourselves as owners and stewards?

But vision can also include a more overarching definition that includes identifying the purpose of the family and the business. What do we want to accomplish through our shared ownership of business assets? What do we and our business stand for? What values do we want to represent and what legacy do we wish pass on to subsequent generations? At the highest level, what is the purpose of our wealth?

One way to approach the creation of a vision is to look at the past. Elements of a family vision are informed by history, both good and bad. If, for instance, there has been animosity or division in the family, the family may be particularly attuned to creating a vision that stresses their commitment to stay together. If they have a strong religious foundation, then their vision will reflect that to a large degree. Historical events help guide and instruct families in the development of their vision of the future.

History and values are central to the Murugappa Group, a Chennai, India-based family business that dates from 1900 and now encompasses more than 28 separate businesses. One of the family members offered this perspective: "We consider ourselves custodians to a heritage and trustees to a tradition, both built on togetherness, trust, mutual respect, ethical values, and, above all, dignity, independence, and discipline. As the scope and magnitude of the family and business leadership changes, we are preparing ourselves for the great challenges ahead."[1] This mentality is shared throughout the family, and provides the impetus for a vision.

Not surprisingly, each family member will interpret history and envision a future that is very personal. The collaborative effort in developing a vision goes a long way in uniting family members around a collective future vision. There are no standards for what should be included in your family vision. The questions you will need to answer in crafting your vision depend upon what is important to your family and your business. However, we will offer some general guidelines and suggestions later in this chapter and provide examples of vision statements that have been drafted by other families.

In our work, we see that many families try to draw a distinction between vision, mission, and purpose, or get caught up in terminology in some other way. They also wrestle with wording and meaning once they agree on a particular terminology. In so doing, some families lose sight of the big picture. In our view, the label is not that important; rather, the *process* of looking inward together and deciding who you are, what you stand for, why you should have a collective aspiration for the future, and where you want to be in the future matter most. Without those guideposts, drawing up an effective continuity plan becomes considerably more difficult, if not impossible. So, call it a vision, mission, purpose, or another label that works for your family. But recognize the importance of discussing and agreeing upon this foundation.

Many families avoid having discussions about vision because they are uncomfortable with disagreement. They don't want to deal with conflict or open up a Pandora's box by acknowledging as a family that they don't all agree upon where they want to go. In this situation, it's helpful to acknowledge that it is better to face the lack of consensus as a group and work toward agreeing upon how to move forward rather than having no discussion at all. (Later in the chapter, we will provide some methodologies that may make this process less threatening.)

Also important is the need to recognize that these are critical questions for individual family members to consider on their own. Everyone has their own personal aspirations and understanding of what the business means to them and what value they derive from being engaged as management, as an owner, and/or as a family member. The challenge of establishing vision is to try to honor individual perspectives within the context of a collective consensus.

Why Is a Vision for the Future So Important?

Some of our clients find it difficult to embrace the practical importance that the development of vision carries. They may see it is an abstract exercise—philosophical in nature, interesting but not particularly useful.

In our experience, an aligned understanding and articulation of the future for the family and the business are critical to successful continuity planning. A clear vision is the bedrock upon which all continuity planning (and other decisions, for that matter) rest. If, for instance, there is a disagreement among family members as to a particular decision or direction the business should take, an agreed-upon vision can be an invaluable reference point and a place of common understanding. Also, remember that a vision is organic in nature. It needs to be revisited as a family evolves from one generation to the next.

One of our associates once worked with a 100-year-old business in which the family was selecting its next CEO. They had always had a family CEO in the past, but at this particular time, the business was going through a challenging transition from one industry to another. They also had a policy stating they should pick the most qualified leader, family member or otherwise. But as they went through the search process for a new CEO, it was clear that the family felt it would lose its connection to the business without a family member as the leader. As a result, they revisited their vision and decided a family leader was important. They also built a management team and board around the new CEO to make sure she was capable of taking the business through the transition.

The lesson here is that there's no one "right" answer. Some families believe family management maintains a family connection so that owners stay interested and the business reflects the family's priorities. Others believe family management causes conflict, or they establish very stringent criteria that define "most qualified." Some have no family in management at all. The key is for the family to have a conversation and get their views on the table so the best decisions for the family and the business can be made.

A strong sense of vision can occasionally take some family businesses in interesting directions. For instance, ABARTA Inc., headquartered in Pittsburgh, PA (now in its third and fourth generations of ownership), emphasizes the overriding importance of integrity in all business matters. That value led the company to fight an antitrust suit rather than accept an out-of-court settlement. Although the company prevailed in court, their legal defense ended up costing them more than what they would have paid to settle the case.

Beyond providing direction for specific family decisions, a shared vision contributes to family unity and connectedness. Benefits include[2]

- **Economic.** A feeling of shared purpose—the sense that coming together will prove financially rewarding—carries obvious economic benefits, since everyone is focused on the objective of financial success. That's particularly the case in challenging economic conditions, where significant obstacles and issues can often bring families closer together. Studies have documented that family-owned businesses often financially outperform other companies. A 2011 study by Credit Suisse and Ernst & Young of members of the Family Business Network International in 33 countries found that family companies were more profitable than public companies in many cases, despite certain economies of scale that researchers expected would work against the family-run enterprises.[3]
- **Sociological.** Here, the question of "Why are we here?" becomes central. A family's vision and purpose can positively impact their community through charitable giving and other community-minded programs. Further, that sense of community focus can help guide future generations as they uphold prior generations' core values.
- **Psychological.** Financial rewards are far from the only reason prompting succeeding generations of family members to bond. A sense of common vision and purpose offers a valuable emotional asset—a feeling of satisfaction, commitment, and group fulfillment. Families stay together because they have certain values that

bind them. Family governance authority James Hughes describes this as a "family of affinity," which is bonded by positive feelings, not merely genetic lineage.[4] Purpose becomes inclusive, not exclusive. Further, those values are principles that guide them in their day-to-day lives and have created a family that they can be proud of. They want to be able to sustain those values.

- **Practical.** Family values and purpose also provide direction in making central practical decisions related to strategy, structure, organization culture, governance, and human capital development, as seen in our example above.

How Family Businesses Put Their Vision into Words

It's essential that a family's vision be drawn up in a document—a clear, easy-to-understand statement and an important reference point for current and future generations. A good time to begin the visioning process is when a new generation of family begins its involvement, either entering management or participating in family or board meetings. The vision should be revisited as each new generation enters, at the very least, and possibly more frequently, depending upon the degree of change in the family and business environments.

To provide a better understanding of the steps involved in developing a vision statement, here are three examples we use in our work with family businesses. While these examples can serve as a valuable reference, we caution that they should not be used as a draft or starting point for your family. Simply reworking the vision of another business robs a family of the opportunity to articulate a unique and meaningful vision.

Example # 1: This family vision statement focuses in large part on the impact of the family. It also emphasizes the vision espoused by the founders of the businesses, one of the reference points for building a vision statement that we referred to earlier in this chapter.

Our family seeks to achieve growth and prosperity through all of our business endeavors, extending well beyond the present generation. We are deeply committed to the cultivation and perpetuation of the entrepreneurial vision of our founders. We seek to provide qualified family members with the opportunity to participate in the family business so that they may find personal fulfillment in their careers, contribute to the family enterprise, and maintain a connection between the values and vision of the family and the business.

We understand that the success of our companies depends upon the contributions of many dedicated people. We will continue to foster the spirit of "extended family" to all of our employees by sharing appreciation, rewards, and benefits that will maximize a mutually prosperous and enriching long-term relationship. We will endeavor to model and teach the Christian beliefs and values to all generations, encouraging them to carry on the Christian traditions of their forefathers.

We will develop consistent and compatible objectives for all family endeavors—business, investment, and philanthropic.

Example #2: This format illustrates the different purpose served by a family mission statement and the business mission statement. It also illustrates that families can have more than one statement if they think that separate documents are appropriate to their situation. As we've mentioned, some families distinguish between the two, while others approach them jointly.

Family

Our mission as a family is to help each other learn and grow in ways that promote happiness in ourselves and those around us, and to be responsible stewards of our family business, so that we might leave the world a better place for future generations.

Business

Our family-owned company will grow as a leading manufacturer and distributor by providing our customers with quality products and superior service for a fair price and profit.

The distinctions between the two statements are evident. The family's statement focuses on themselves, their community, and their desire to improve the world around them for generations to come. The business statement emphasizes quality of product and service in exchange for a reasonable profit. That said, the statements are not conflicting; both support the importance of balancing the needs of all stakeholders, including owners, customers, and the broader community.

Example #3: This statement addresses ownership issues and priorities and sets expectations for owners' commitment to the business.

Our vision is to build a healthy, growing, successful, private, family-owned business by doing whatever it takes to assure the best possible environment for the respect and dignity of our people. We set excellence as our standard for ownership:

- *to know the executive team well and comfortably*
- *to have a most special relationship with the president*
- *to be always aware of the key issues and key decisions— never being surprised where it's important*
- *to know how we stack up against the best all over the world*
- *to assure all in the organization that we are highly engaged and committed*
- *to enjoy working together as brothers*

Again, values are central to this mission statement. Mentioning the importance of respect and dignity for people clarifies the value that the family places on how it treats employees. Additionally, the statement emphasizes the importance of remaining a private company, with family members likely occupying key leadership positions.

These samples demonstrate the varied ways in which a vision statement can take shape. Some families create a lengthy and highly detailed document, while others may capture their family's purpose and intent in a few simple sentences. There is not any right way to express a vision. Focus on what matters to your family, be it a prosperous organization, a company that genuinely values everyone who works there, or a commitment to the community around you.

Keep in mind that a vision is more than just a declaration. It serves as a foundation for significant decisions and behavior. An articulated vision is inspirational, instructive, and serves as a roadmap through the multitude of decisions encompassed in continuity planning, for both the family and the business.

The Importance of Values

In addition to an articulated vision, values represent an important element of continuity. It is important to recognize the distinct difference between vision and values. Values guide day-to-day behavior, while a vision is a desired long-term outcome. Awareness of that distinction helps families appreciate both, and in so doing, makes drawing up separate vision and values statements that much easier should the family decide that two distinct documents are important.

With regard to values, so many decisions that a family makes about themselves and their business are influenced by values that have guided the family for generations. And, as part of continuity planning, families will often identify and articulate these in a statement of values, as a point of clarity but also as a starting point in developing guidelines for generational transitions. If senior-generation members see that important family values carry on through the next generation, it reduces the current generation's anxiety about ceding control and contributes to a collaborative effort in realizing a future vision. Values help cement a variety of essential attributes. They provide

- a basis for corporate culture,
- a template for decision-making,

- a means of challenging conventional thinking,
- a means of inspiring exceptional performance,
- a means of improving strategic planning.[5]

Family values help build a bridge between the goals of the family and the business, and can also create synergies and complementarities between the family and the business. And, if shared values are in place, a family is aware of the importance of passing on them on to subsequent generations.

Here are two examples of value statements:

Example #1

Family Values Statement
Mutual respect, honesty, and integrity are basic elements of our family and business relationships. Without these, we cannot achieve our vision and mission.

Faith
We believe in living and abiding by the principles of our faith.

Family
We are deeply committed to promoting and perpetuating the unity of our family.

Philanthropy
We support and encourage philanthropy with both time and treasure.

Individuality
We respect and celebrate the special purpose, uniqueness, and freedom of each individual spirit.

Community
We will be good, law-abiding citizens to our community and country. We support the perpetuation of the free enterprise system.

Productivity

We value a strong, proactive work ethic for a fulfilling life.

Education

We believe knowledge and education empower individuals to grow and achieve their dreams.

Example #2

Family Values and Mission Statement

To plant the seeds of excellence and to perpetuate a commitment to family, which fosters love, trust, respect and honor.

As a family we strive to
act with integrity,
promote self-esteem,
teach "sense of family,"
pursue the love of work,
cherish individuality, independent thinking, freedom of choice,
encourage the participation and empowerment of every family member,
commit to communication and the resolution of conflicts,
serve as responsible "role models" of productive and creative people,
create wealth responsibly and confront the challenges of wealth,
acknowledge excellence as a personal expression, with freedom to learn from mistakes,
demonstrate proactive compassion and generosity,
focus energy on the enhancement of our community, and
create an environment of lifelong learning.
All these to we aspire to pass on and teach from generation to generation.

Those are not abstract pronouncements. Consider Lichtenstein-based Hilti, a family-owned business that manufactures construction, building maintenance, and mining industries products. Upon receiving the prestigious Carl Bertelsmann Prize in 2003 for innovative solutions, the

Bertelsmann Foundation specifically cited Hilti's focus on values that are embraced throughout the organization: "Hilti employees live out its principles in their daily work."

Incoming generations benefit from developing alignment around family values. Cousin groups are more diverse than sibling teams, where shared values may be fostered by growing up together. Subsequent generations have different parents, who model and advocate values that are uniquely theirs. It is important to create opportunities for the next generation to establish consensus on what values will shape their behavior and decisions as they move forward. In addition to creating a bond within the group, they will also be influenced by those values when developing their own vision for the future. What is more, the articulation of shared values is also a means for honoring the legacy of the family and business. Often, the values articulated by a cousin generation will reflect the lessons and experiences passed down by prior generations.

Additionally, shared values can help put continuity issues in their most effective chronological order. Many families get hung up on tactical topics surrounding continuity, only to skip essential questions, such as whether the family always wants to have a family member at the head of the company. If, on the other hand, agreed-upon values and purpose have already addressed these sorts of issues, decisions are subsequently that much easier to address.

How Families Craft Their Vision and Values Statements

Vision and values statements are highly personal and are specific to the collective view of the family. However, as important as the statement is the process by which they are created. A beautifully descriptive statement means nothing if family members have not gone through the process of creating it as a group, mulling over the meaning of the words they choose, gaining consensus on a future together, and understanding the implications of the decisions they are making.

Because the process of collaborating is as important as the output, we advocate creating vision and values statements by working together in person and including as many family members as possible. Although, as we have pointed out, vision and values are two very separate types of statements, coming together as a group and engaging in frank and open discussion is the key to successfully drawing up both documents. Group discussion is not easy for all family members, some of whom may feel uncomfortable sharing their opinion in a family meeting. This is true for a number of reasons: they may be intimidated by other family members (sometimes in leadership roles in the business); they may feel that because they don't work in the business, their opinion is less important; they may have some anxiety over one or two family members who might be triggered by others' perceptions and lose their temper; or they may just generally feel uncomfortable sharing their opinion about the business and the family in front of others, particularly when it is a new experience. We encourage families to ensure that they are doing whatever they can to create an inclusive, comfortable environment for all participants.

The first step in designing the drafting process is determining who will be involved. With smaller family groups, it is often feasible to invite every family member. By contrast, if a family is particularly large or diverse, it may be more practical to limit participants (for instance, selecting representatives from each generation or family group, or the family council). Additionally, a family may wish to consider trusted nonfamily advisers or management who have played a pivotal role in their business (an extended family of sorts). Again, this decision is highly personal—some will opt to include any number of people outside the family, while others will want to limit the process to family members exclusively.

As to the logistics of the meeting, it is essential to gather everyone together outside of the confines of the working day. It may be after hours or a weekend retreat, when other responsibilities and obligations do not intrude on the discussion and decision-making process.

Know, too, that it is often not possible to draft a statement that everyone is comfortable signing off on in a single meeting. Coming to agreement may require several gatherings, particularly if there are significant points of disagreement. The key is not to rush the process. Not only will your statement benefit from a sufficient investment of time, it's less likely that any person in the group will feel pushed into a decision with which they didn't agree. Another helpful tip to gain buy-in from large family groups is to provide a mechanism for broad input to a draft. If the family group is so large that all cannot participate in the drafting process, all members should have an opportunity to review a draft before it is final and to make suggestions.

It can be helpful to kick-start people's thinking prior to meeting to draft the actual statement by suggesting topics that can help participants gather their thoughts prior to a group discussion. Along those lines, here's a sample questionnaire that can be distributed prior to a family meeting:

Where Are We Going with This Company?

Discussion Preparation

In ten years...

- What is the desired state of ownership (in terms of family and generational control)?
- What are our expectations about family members in leadership? Will a family member necessarily occupy the CEO position?
- What aspirations do we have in terms of the size of the business, market penetration, the number of markets served, and concentration versus diversification?

*As we think about owning a durable and healthy
enterprise...*

- How do we envision the financial health and performance of the company?
  - markets served, considering the sustainability of those markets
  - sales growth rate
  - profitability ratios
  - dividends/return on investment
  - other measures
- What is our approach to risk-taking going forward and use of debt to fund growth and new opportunities?
- What culture are we trying to promote and grow in our family enterprise? What underlying values do we hold that will drive that culture?
- Accountability is a concept that ties directly to culture. What will we mean by accountability as we implement our desired culture?

Questions for Vision Sessions

A family's vision statement is a personal document, one that reflects family values and personal, branch, and collective aspirations (which can be quite diverse). But, as a general rule, there are certain questions that can be posed in the process that may prove particularly helpful. Here are a number of questions that may prove valuable as you discuss your own values and purpose statement, many of which take issues raised in the pre-meeting questionnaire we just cited and break them down even further:

- **Do we want to stay together?** As we mentioned earlier, some families are taken aback by this question, but it needs to be posed nonetheless. While it may be assumed, it's important to establish that some members of the family group do, in fact, wish to remain together. It may come as a surprise that some do not. As a matter of planning, that's an essential point to establish upfront. You might also ask family members to consider and articulate the circumstances under which the business would be sold in the future. Might it be if no family members work in the business? Or if no family member is available or equipped to lead the business? Is there a specific selling price that would trigger divestiture?

- **If we want to stay in business together, how will we transfer ownership to the next generation?** How would we feel if 20 percent of the next-generation members decided that they wanted to sell their shares? And does "transfer" mean a gift, or do we expect the next generation to buy the business? Can we afford such a request?

- **Who can be an owner?** What about family members not working in the business? What about in-laws? Would we ever share ownership with key nonfamily employees?

- **What do we want ownership to look like?** For instance: "We want a collective future ownership that provides the freedom, benefits, and opportunities to meet owners' individual and collective needs." How will we draw the line between ownership and management? Will we hold shares in trust or outright?

- **How do we want the company to be led?** How important is it that someone with the family name leads the company? How would we feel if an outsider or inside nonfamily member was head of the company? Is it the chair position or the CEO position that is most important? What philosophy of leadership works best? What would we do if some family members proved to be ineffective leaders?

- **What do we want the business to look like?** Do we envision a multisector enterprise over time, or will we focus on our current industry indefinitely? How comfortable would we be with diversification? What shape might that diversification take (diversified product lines or services, geographic diversification, unrelated diversification in other lines of business in other industries)?

- **What would we do if we could not compete in the market that we are in now?** What would we do if our business became outdated? Would we sell the business or would we just go into a new business? How would we feel if, to take advantage of a significant opportunity, we needed to give up a portion of family ownership? Would we be comfortable trading an element of family control to raise capital? Under what circumstances?

- **If we have been debt averse in the past, how would we feel if we needed to take on significant debt in the future?** How would this decision be made (solely by owners, by the board, by management, for example)? How would we include family owners in this significant decision? What if some family members were strongly opposed to the idea?

- **How would we feel if we had to reduce financial benefits to family members in order to grow or even survive?** Again, who would make this decision? What criteria would be used to make the decision? How would family owners participate in the decision?

- **What if a next-generation member came to us with an idea to start an entirely new business?** How would we evaluate the opportunity? Who would be involved? What role would the rest of the family play in the decision?

- **How much information should we share?** For instance, should family meeting deliberations be captured in minutes and distributed? If so, with whom? How should financial information from the company be distributed and to whom?

- **What do we want governance to look like?** Will we have a family decision-making body that is active? How will the people who participate in governance be selected?

One final question warrants special attention:

- **When we have had differences in the past, what has brought us together?** What resonates with us? This can prove a great rallying point, particularly in situations in which family members are disagreeing or expressing discontent. Put another way, what bonds us? What do we as family members experience that an outsider could not?

Not only can discussion of that question bring family members together on a common point, it also helps reinforce the strong feeling that family members can have about their business. It is not merely a business, but also an emotional bond with loved ones. The family feels obligated to move the business forward and hand it off to the next generation in better shape than when they first received it (or at least preserve it). The business is in their DNA. To some extent, it is a reflection of themselves, and in some cases even defines them.

To that end, it can be helpful to encourage family members to share a story or anecdote that illustrates what they feel is the family's rallying point. Put another way, what memories do they have of why they all started (or work in) this business in the first place? These contributions can help strengthen the value of those experiences that truly resonate with everyone.

These kinds of questions underscore the message that a family business is certainly a financial entity, an opportunity that many others cannot access. But it is also an opportunity for self and collective pride, shared meaning and identity. And, in its own way, that is as valuable as any form of financial benefit.

Questions for Values Sessions

The methodology for drafting a values statement is not that different from that of a vision statement. It is important to be inclusive, to take adequate time, and to encourage discussion on a variety of viewpoints from a diverse group of participants.

Like a vision session, it can also be very helpful to incorporate some carefully crafted questions to kick-start the overall discussion. Given that these questions are geared to values rather than vision, the focus is obviously a bit different. Here are several examples:

1. Note one or two things that you think our family does very, very well.
2. What are the central values of our family? How can these values be preserved for the future?
3. What family values would you want to see perpetuated / reflected in the company?
4. What makes us proud to be owners of this business?

These sample questions illustrate the kinds of issues that should be examined when drafting a values statement. On a broader scale, ask yourself and others: What makes this company, this family, and the relationship that we share valuable to us? What ideals and principles do we hold that are important enough that we want to pass them along to subsequent generations? Allow plenty of time to discuss these critical questions in your family meetings. If you have a large family, these questions are often best addressed in small groups (four or five people), who then report back to the larger family during the meeting.

How to Make Decisions

Decision-making for business-owning families requires very careful thought. It is important that the family reflect on its history of decision-making and think about what should be sustained and what should change.

Smaller families may hope for unanimous approval, while large groups may opt for a vote and set a target for approval of a majority or supermajority.

One good option is to aspire to consensus, where consensus is defined as all group members agreeing to follow a course of action, even though some members may not fully agree with the decision itself.

Following discussion, one way of measuring consensus is to ask all members whether they support the decision, are against it (but are willing to go along with the decision), object (cannot agree to go along with the decision), or choose to abstain. Then, take a straw poll. If there are no objections, you can choose to move forward to the next item. If there are objections, the objecting party is required to propose a change or modification.

Of course, there's certainly the chance that some members of the group are particularly strident in their opposition to a certain issue. In that instance, it becomes critical that the process not come to a grinding halt. That can be especially frustrating when only a small number of the group hold up progress through their opposition and, in effect, create a "majority of one."

One way to address this is to turn to a simple majority vote. Another is to defer the decision to senior members of the group. A third option is to bring in an outside facilitator who can work as an impartial guide to help bring varied opinions together.

In a large or divisive group, there is value to considering a democratic process—whatever side of an issue gets the most votes carries the day. If this process is suited to your situation, consider:

- Does everyone get a vote?
- Will votes be counted by the person or by the shares a person owns in the company?
- Should married couples be counted as one vote so as not to put singles at a disadvantage?
- Should a supermajority (65 to 75 percent) be necessary to approve an issue?
- What sorts of provisions should be available to break ties?
- Who will take responsibility for guiding the decision-making process? Will it be the group as a whole or, alternately, the person who suggests a particular topic or issue?

- Is it a level playing field? For example, will younger family members be permitted to submit their opinions, with elder-generation members having the final say on an issue?

While the process of achieving consensus on a vision or values statement may sound complicated, the great news is that defining a decision-making rule will serve the family well in the future. Undoubtedly the family will face a myriad of decisions in the continuity planning process for which it will need to decide "how it decides." The creation of vision and values statements allows the family to practice decision-making and craft a process that works for them. These statements also play a significant role in creating a perception of safety among family members—a personal need for most of us.

Here is one specific example of how a family handled the process. When the Andrews family—a group of third-generation owners and their spouses—decided to develop a family vision statement to provide direction to their newly created independent board of directors, they knew that the input of the full family group would be critical to success. Luckily, the family had a mechanism to gain that input: its twice-yearly family meeting. At this meeting, 12 cousins and their spouses gathered to discuss issues relevant to their ownership of their family enterprise. With our support, the family members held a two-hour session to create a first draft of their vision statement. The process worked as follows:

1. Family members were posed a series of questions to which they responded individually:
   a. What should we own together?
   b. Who should own the business?
   c. How should family be involved?
   d. What financial return should the business generate?
2. Family members were arranged into groups with a diversity of age, gender, outright ownership and in-laws; employed and nonemployed; and family branch representation to discuss their individual answers.

3. Each group (four to five people) wrote down their areas of consensus and areas in which they had a diversity of opinion, and presented this feedback to the full group.
4. The feedback of all the groups was taken by the family council to synthesize into a draft of areas of agreement and areas for future discussion.
5. At the next family meeting, the group discussed the draft (which was sent out in advance) and created a revised version.
6. At a family meeting, one year from the commencement of the process, the final version was approved by a vote of the family and submitted to the board of directors.

The details of this process can be adjusted by family—what questions to pose, who to include in the conversation, how many drafts are required to gain final approval—but the process itself can be useful to families of any size.

The Value of Ground Rules for Family Interaction

No matter the procedure you select to make decisions, it can be very helpful to lay out a few meeting ground rules for family interaction at the outset. Not only can such rules make the process considerably more constructive and efficient, they can also head off potential problems well before they crop up and disrupt your work.

Here are some ground rules to consider:

- Be sure there are no surprise issues. Everyone who takes part in the process knows the issues beforehand and his or her charge to reach a decision.
- Identify conflicts of interest. Any personal interests or agendas are disclosed beforehand.
- Encourage an atmosphere of respect. Each participant feels respected and heard. Focus on issues, not personalities.

- Be inclusive. Work to encourage input from as many as possible.
- Encourage a sense of mutual commitment. A genuine effort is made to find a "win-win" solution before a vote or decision.
- Find a sense of closure. A formal decision on the entire document prior to the close of the meeting should be necessary to ensure all are in agreement.
- Review.   Everyone has an opportunity to offer a frank critique of the process.
- Communicate with others. Assign responsibility for communicating decisions to those affected who did not participate in the decision-making process.
- Honor each other's time by paying full attention. No cell phones allowed. Unless it's absolutely necessary, leave the room only at breaks.

Similar to setting a decision-making process, establishing a set of ground rules will serve the family well as it dives into the continuity planning process. The rules should be applicable to any family interaction. And, to be effective, family members must agree to the rules, both to follow them and to police the group to ensure they are adhered to. Some clients require family members to sign a document that lists the ground rules to signal their commitment. In others, lighthearted but effective processes are used to ensure adherence, such as a minimal fine for a member not following the rules (the money may go into a fund to give to a charity or to fund a family award or fun event). In some cases, uncooperative family members are rewarded a rubber chicken or some other gag gift as a "prize."

One important issue to bear in mind in the process itself recognizes the likelihood that not everyone is going to wholly agree with every element of every decision made. As we have noted, vision and values are very personal considerations. Not everyone is going to feel exactly the same way. Moreover, the larger and more diverse the group, the greater the likelihood of significantly different opinions and perspectives.

With that issue in mind, it is also important to embrace the fact that making everyone in the family happy can't necessarily be an objective of the vision and values decision-making process. It is simply not practical. That's why it is so critical to have methodologies in place to help address significant roadblocks. Someone voicing a simple yes or no is one thing; having them say they're not happy about a particular decision, but they can certainly live with it is another matter entirely.

That also underscores the importance of the process itself and not just the document that emerges at the other end. Your objective is to develop a sense of the collective built on the family members' passions and priorities. The rule of thumb is that decisions are made in the best interests of the family, not necessarily any one individual. The stronger the environment of trust, of the family coming together to identify what matters the most to them as a group and a commitment to positioning those values and purposes to help steward the business forward into the future, the more rewarding and successful the process will likely be.

Management consultant David Maister points out that trust can only be earned and deserved through concrete action. Within the context of drawing up vision and values statements, trust is achieved when members of the group are willing to concede certain points or issues for the benefit of the greater good. You don't have to be happy about it, but you are willing to live with it. That, in turn, helps cement trust in others to work for a strong collective vision.

The Evolution of Vision and Values

Family vision and values statements are highly personal documents focused on those specific issues and ideas that matter most to the family. It is not a matter of copying another family's statement or of one family member (or worse a nonfamily member) drawing up a document and everyone else dutifully signing it. It needs to be addressed collectively in as thoughtful and constructive a manner as possible. In addition to other benefits, smooth and effective continuity from one generation to the next depends on it. At the very least, it helps equip the next generation of family and business leaders to carry the torch with something tangible—an articulated set of values as well as an agreed-upon future vision.

Because the business and the context within which it operates change, it is important to review your vision and values periodically, particularly as the business passes from one generation to the next, giving some thought as to whether the vision or values need to be adjusted or refreshed. A new generation may have passions and priorities not shared by preceding generations. It is essential to incorporate those, not merely from the perspective of how they will influence the business but as the means through which they will plan to pass them along to the subsequent generation.

It is also important to recognize that values and vision are organic and evolve from one generation to another. There is no cause to feel guilty or to pass judgment on a particular value or a vision that is no longer appropriate. For instance, one generation may have emphasized the growth of the business above all, while the next generation places greater value on work / life balance. Another example is equality. In sibling generations, many families value equality above all. This can lead to things like paying all siblings in the business the same salary even if they don't have similar positions or levels of authority. Over time, the value of equality gives way to the value of fairness, which may be very different— paying someone what a job is worth so as not to upset the overall pay scale of the company, or focusing on equality at the ownership level rather than at the employee level by gifting children equal shares of stock. In one example, a family agreed that the current generation would retain the same pay level, but that the next generation would have an employment policy that required family to adhere to the pay scale of the business.

It happens all the time with family businesses of all sorts. An old value or vision simply no longer fits. It's okay to move on.

With family vision and values statements in place, it's now time to put them to practical use. First on the list is planning for continuity in business ownership, specifically the role of a vision statement in effectively transferring ownership from one person or group to another.

In Brief

- A shared vision provides the foundation for successful continuity planning.
- Vision can be defined as a family's desired outcome for the business and for themselves as owners and stewards.
- A family must articulate its vision in its own words. While it is helpful to look at examples from other families, it's imperative that families develop their own vision.
- Values are also an important component in continuity in helping guide day-to-day decisions.
- Vision and values evolve. What was appropriate for one generation might not be for another.

3

Ownership Continuity

Many families planning for the future of their business do not give a lot of conscious thought to family values or a vision for the future. In some cases, family members downplay the importance of developing statements that reflect the family's wishes and beliefs. Similarly, ownership continuity planning is often not given the focus it deserves. The end result—as well as the process of ownership continuity planning—is also often perceived as obvious, in that family members think ownership transitions are fairly straightforward. Often they are not, once family members consider of the questions that arise through this important process. While there are many nuances, an ownership continuity plan addresses three specific questions:

- Who will own this business in the future?
- How will ownership be transferred?
- When will ownership be transferred?

In earlier generations, the assumption that the family owns the business and will always own the business is pervasive. This view is one of the reasons why families often pay little attention to ownership continuity planning.

However, like failing to articulate vision and values, failing to plan for ownership continuity can be a costly oversight. It is a critical step in ensuring the overall stability of any family-owned business, and helps family members prepare for their future—in fact, it prompts them to do so.

One stumbling block in considering the issue of continuity of ownership is that many families fail to draw a clear distinction between ownership and leadership succession. This is particularly true in the early stages of a business. Often, when family members address the issue of continuity, the focus is exclusively on leadership—who will run the business now and in the future.

That is a perfectly understandable—and, to a certain degree, sensible—frame of mind. But ownership succession is at least as critical; in fact, it is very much parallel to leadership. As leadership moves from one group to the next, serious thought must be given to who will receive ownership and when and how it will be received. As you will see in some of our examples in this chapter, these decisions are inextricably linked.

Why Does Ownership Continuity Deserve Our Attention?

One reason why ownership continuity needs to be addressed early in a business' growth is that many family members will, naturally enough, have different interpretations of ways to approach ownership. For instance, if there are three children in a particular generation and only one goes into the business, some families feel that child should be made the sole owner, or at least, have ownership control. They believe that child shouldn't have to worry about others who aren't actually involved in the business telling them what to do. On the other hand, many families feel all children should benefit financially from the business, whether they are involved or not. They might receive nonvoting shares or fewer shares than those who are active in the business. But, we often see families give equal shares to those working and not working in the business. They see ownership and management as two fundamentally different topics. Ownership is conferred because you are a member of the family. A leadership position is earned through education and hard work.

Conflict related to ownership transition can be costly or, at the very least, needlessly distracting. South Korea's Samsung Electronics is a case in point. Chairman Lee Kun Hee has transformed his family's dried fish and produce company into the world's biggest maker of televisions and mobile phones. However, he recently had to contend with lawsuits filed by two siblings who argued they failed to receive shares due to them upon their father's death in 1987. Although Hee ultimately prevailed—a South Korean District Court ruled in 2013 that the ten-year period for inheritance claims had already expired—the squabble, if nothing else, generated a swath of negative publicity.

Family members may also have philosophical differences around how ownership is transitioned. Should next-generation members receive stock as a gift, or should they buy the company from the elder generation? The funds from a purchase may be needed to support the elder generation in retirement. Even if the retiring generation does not need the capital generated by selling shares, some families feel that the next generation will take their ownership more seriously if they have to commit capital.

The timing of ownership transition can also foster great debate within the family, between family and management, and between family and advisers. Some families believe in making small gifts of shares to their children at a young age, even if the shares are controlled through a trust. Others want to wait to see whether children will show interest and capability to be involved in the business before they consider transferring shares.

These philosophical differences can be a source of very interesting and lively discussions. What if a family has children who are deemed incapable of running the business or have no interest in joining? What if a family member divorces a spouse who is working in the business? Are children from blended families, adopted or not, eligible to be owners? What about children with special needs? These and other dynamics provide good reason for addressing the issue of ownership as early as possible. As a business and family grow, the issue only becomes more complicated. And, reaching agreement on who is eligible for ownership before the decision applies to specific owners can avoid hurt feelings.

Our general rule of thumb for all complex issues faced by families is for them to consider the implications of their choices and develop guidelines before they are actually needed. Then, when the time comes, an objective decision can be made within an established and agreed-upon process. A simple example: if you decide that allowing spouses to own shares is not something that fits with your family's vision and values, state that rule before there are any spouses eligible for ownership within a specific generation. As in all family business cases, what starts out to be simple is rarely so in the end. So, when you state spouses can't own shares, you need to think about the impact that might have on the development of wills within the family. In the common scenario in which the first to die in a marriage leaves their assets to the remaining spouse, treatment of shares in the business can be tricky. Should those shares go to your children? Should they be available for purchase by the remaining shareholders? If so, how will the price be determined?

Addressing Ownership Continuity

Although ownership continuity is an important issue to take on, it is not an easy or straightforward task. Complexities come from a number of sources—philosophical differences, legal and financial consequences of ownership, the composition of the ownership and management groups, differing risk profiles and desire for liquidity across owners conflict within the family. These are just some of the factors that affect ownership continuity. One of the greatest barriers to addressing ownership continuity is an emotional one, because it forces the family to address mortality. No one wants to ask Dad how he plans to pass down his shares. It can seem greedy and mercenary. One family with whom we worked used the euphemism "taking out the trash" to describe their father's passing away! It was too upsetting for them to actually use the term dying. When they discussed what actions they would take after their father's passing, they said, "When dad takes out the trash, we will…"

Imagine this scenario. An estate planner arranges a meeting supposedly involving both the parents and the children. The wrinkle is, the parents don't attend. At the outset of the meeting, the planner announces to the next generation that their father is dead (he's not, of course) and asks the children what they are going to do. They then run an exercise to try to figure out what important decisions will need to be made to pass ownership to their generation.

Although the session is designed to encourage family members to start thinking about ownership succession and the necessary steps and tools that need to be in place beforehand, it occasionally doesn't go over that well. In one family who were working with their estate planning advisers, the kids were offended by the ersatz death announcement. They felt set up and manipulated, and further, believed it was disrespectful to their father. The approach derailed the entire conversation. Yet their father had thought it was a great idea and supported the process when his financial advisers suggested it.

The timing of the transition to next-generation owners is an interesting decision for current owners. With leadership succession, there is often a concrete point when you recognize the time has come to prepare for that transition—someone is getting ready to retire, so we need to think about who will take their place. By contrast, there is often not a defined point when it becomes clear that ownership transition must be addressed. And, in fact, many elder-generation members want to hold onto their shares as long as possible. If they have retired from a management position, the ownership stake can give them a sense that they are still part of the business.

The trend toward having children later in life further complicates ownership transition. The current generation may not be comfortable passing on shares until the younger generation demonstrates maturity in their financial decisions or possibly an interest in entering the business. If children are not reaching the age of 30 until their parents are 60 or beyond, this demographic trend supports the desire to hold onto shares longer. In some cases, that might prompt the next generation to feel underappreciated, distrusted, or even unwelcome in the business.

Ownership transition decisions cannot always be undone. When a family decides that it is important to have a family leader of the business, this decision can be revisited. Ownership succession decisions do not always allow for easy adjustments across generations. Often, trusts established at one stage of a business are difficult to undo later on. Further, decisions to gift only to those involved in the business or to maintain strong family branch representation in ownership can have significant consequences down the road. If you decide to give shares only to family members in the business, what happens when you have a son who has no children, or who has children who aren't capable of working in the business? On the other hand, what if children in the third generation are highly qualified and would work well within the business, but they don't have any shares in their branch of the family because their father was not involved in the business? These and other issues make it important to consider the implications of the who, how, and when decisions in ownership transition, not just for their immediate effect but also with regard to the impact for generations to come.

Due to the variety of factors that influence the ownership transition decision—both philosophical (how you treat your children) and practical (tax liability and legal matters, among others)—it's important to involve a variety of people in the decision-making process, including tax professionals, legal counsel, and financial advisers.

And, while the financial consequences of ownership transition are important, it is important not to lose sight of the impact those decisions will have on the well-being, happiness, and harmony of the family. We believe it is essential to keep those considerations foremost in your mind. To illustrate: you may make certain decisions that save millions of dollars in taxes, but if those savings come at the expense of alienating family members whom you value, is the money saved really worth it? This consideration highlights the importance of establishing a clear vision and set of values prior to embarking on ownership continuity planning. It also highlights the importance of inclusion. If you are senior-generation owners, get next-generation family members involved in the ownership transition process with you. In our experience, ownership transitions that come as a surprise to next-generation family members are already fraught with potential conflicts. Good and bad surprises are unpleasant when we're grieving over the loss of a family member; try to avoid such an emotional outcome.

The Basic Questions of Ownership

Ownership continuity planning addresses a fundamental question: who do we feel should own this business in the future? It also touches on the intertwined questions of when and how ownership will be transitioned. These questions encompass a variety of fundamental issues, many related to the family's vision and values:

- **What value do we place on working in the business?** Do we only give shares to those who are employed in the business? What if we are ready to pass on shares before we know who will work in the business? What if those working in the business leave by choice, or are terminated?
- **How do we view the issue of equality?** Should all family members receive an equal number of shares? Or, could we create equality among our children by passing on other nonbusiness assets we hold?
- **How do we view the emotional ramifications of these decisions?** How and when should we communicate the message to a child who is receiving fewer shares than his siblings?
- **How long do we want our legacy to last?** Should we be more concerned about passing shares to future generations or providing a solid financial return to the current generation? Is there a trade-off?
- **When will the current generation be ready to give up some control over decision-making?** Retired leaders often like to maintain an interest in the business so they can have some degree of influence. Should prudent tax planning outweigh the desire to remain involved?
- **When will the next generation be prepared to take on the important responsibilities of ownership?** How can we best prepare them for these responsibilities? What

criteria need to be met in order for the senior generation to feel comfortable? Who decides on those criteria?

- **What if the next generation does not show an interest in the business?** Are we willing to let leadership pass into the hands of a nonfamily member, or would we prefer to sell? How should this decision be made?
- **How important is it that the family owns all the stock in the business?** Some families are willing to share ownership with outsiders to bring new money into the business. Others want 100 percent control. Outsiders can lend funding and expertise, but decision-making becomes more complicated when ownership in divided between family and nonfamily owners.
- **Is it feasible to pass shares to the next generation through gifting, or is it preferable to have the next generation buy the business from the current generation, from a tax-planning standpoint or to provide retirement income to the elder generation?** What emotional considerations are involved in a gift versus a purchase?

Some families separate ownership into voting and nonvoting shares. While this structure can prove an effective estate planning strategy that allows the older generation to retain control while passing on economic benefits to subsequent generations, the decision can also carry an implicit message that the older generation doesn't trust younger family members enough to take part in voting decisions. That can make younger family members feel entirely powerless, leaving them to ask themselves "What do I really own here? If I have no control, what's the point of my participation? When will I be considered credible enough to have a vote?"

One family with whom we have worked has four owners in their fifties running the business. When asked what the "owners" wanted for the future of the business, they consistently deferred to three older family members, all of whom were in their eighties. On the surface, this deference made no sense. The four people running the business were doing a very good job. The three older family members agreed their performance was top-notch.

It all had to do with the structure of ownership. While the elder generation had gifted all nonvoting shares to the succeeding generation, comprising 90 percent of the total ownership, the three older family members owned 100 percent of the voting shares. So, they had the final say. This power was strengthened by a statement in the bylaws granting voting shareholders the authority to approve any decision involving $1 million or more (this in a company with $500 million in annual revenue).

Consider the ramifications of this arrangement. For one thing, even relatively modest financial decisions had to go through the older family members. That often compromised management's ability to make efficient decisions. Just as important, what sort of message did that convey to the four people actually running the business? Deep down, did it suggest that the older family members didn't feel comfortable trusting the next generation to make reasoned decisions?

The Value of Shareholder Agreements

One strategy that is useful in mapping out the specifics of shareholder ownership—and, in so doing, effectively addressing the questions and issues we just presented—is discussing and drafting a shareholder agreement. This document, as the name implies, lays out the specifics of a variety of shareholder-related issues. We should note that some people call shareholder agreements stock transfer agreements or buy-sell agreements. Like other documents and agreements that impact both the family and the business, it's important that consensus be reached so that everyone effectively buys into the guidelines specified in the agreement. In the case of a shareholder agreement, approval by all owners is imperative. The document is only legally binding upon those who sign. So, most families will not enter into an agreement unless all owners sign.

Although the process is very personal, it can be helpful to gain a sense of the sorts of issues that may be worth addressing. Presented below is a questionnaire we have used with clients in the past.

Shareholder Agreement Discussion Questions

A. **Purpose**
   - What are the primary goals we hope to achieve through a shareholder agreement?

B. **Who can own shares?**
   1. Should we limit the number of shareholders?
   2. What are the requirements of shareholders?
      a) educational level?
      b) working in the business?
      c) age?
   3. Should we use voting, nonvoting stock?
   4. Can adopted children, in-laws, nonfamily employees own? Are there any limitations? How do we deal with wills that transfer assets to the remaining spouse?
   5. Can a trust hold stock?
   6. Should family branch ownership be maintained in subsequent generations? (e.g., 33 percent ownership in the hands of descendants of each of three second-generation owners?)
   7. Should the CEO own a certain percentage?
   8. What is the maximum percentage owned by a single shareholder?
   9. Can someone buy back in after they have sold shares?

C. **How and when is stock given, bought, and sold?**
   1. When does the company have the right to buy back stock?
      a) in the case of disability (permanent)?
      b) in the event of involuntary termination?
      c) in case of divorce?

2. When must it buy back stock?
   a) in the event of disability
   b) in the event of death
3. How will the company fund buyouts?
   a) Will life insurance policies be secured to fund buyouts at death?
   b) What is the maximum dollar amount or percentage of shares the company will buy back in a given year?
   c) If the company cannot buy back all shares, will it pay interest to the selling party until the buyout is complete?
4. To whom can owners sell? swap with?
   a) How frequently can they sell/swap?
   b) What percentage must one sell?
   c) What special circumstances determine this? (i.e., divorce, disability, retirement)
5. Valuation: What processes are to be used? (formula versus appraisal?)
   a) What is the update frequency?
   b) What will be the discounts?
   c) What is the definition of market value?
   d) What process is used if the valuation is contested?
6. Notification: How and when does a shareholder make known that they want to sell? ?
7. Is a noncompete and/or nonsolicitation of employees required if a family member exits ownership?
8. What happens if the business or a family member defaults on payment to purchase shares?
9. Is there an age at which owners must sell?

D. **Other Items**
   1. Should a look back clause be included to compensate a selling shareholder in the event that the shareholder sells a block of shares at a specified price and subsequently a higher value is established?
   2. Are there deadlock provisions?

3. Are prenuptial agreements required for next-generation shareholders before shares are gifted to them?
4. What happens to unneeded insurance?
5. If the business is held in an S-Corp, is it mandatory that the business distribute cash to owners to pay taxes? How will the rate of the tax distribution be determined?
6. Can owners borrow against the stock (e.g., use their stock as collateral for a loan)?

While owners may have different feelings about shareholder agreements (see possible concerns below), we strongly believe that such an agreement is imperative to ensuring ownership continuity. And, we believe it is important to implement one relatively early in a company's life span. For one thing, owners—both existing and prospective—become familiar with the agreement that much sooner. They are fully apprised of what they can and cannot do with regard to the shares that they own. And, the earlier the issue is considered in a company's life span, the fewer people are involved in the approval process.

Another consideration to bear in mind is the inherently restrictive nature of shareholder agreements. Although they lay out a variety of issues that impact shareholder ownership, a basic tenet of many such agreements concerns controlling to whom you may sell shares and to whom you may not. That can make perfect sense—after all, you don't want a disgruntled family member selling their shares to a major competitor. While these protections are important, asking owners to take on restrictions that may reduce the value of their ownership is a difficult proposition. Conceptually, it makes less economic sense (to shareholders seeking liquidity) to impose such restrictions, yet you can imagine the consequences of the absence of specific rules around divestitures.

Often, the most controversial element of the shareholder agreement is the valuation methodology—at what value will my shares be redeemed should I choose to sell? Owners of privately held family businesses should be aware of discounts to share value taken for lack of liquidity and control. For those who are not aware of the valuation process, the term "discount" refers to the fact that shares in a family-owned business are valued less (or discounted) than the value of shares in a similar publicly traded company.

With respect to a discount for lack of liquidity, as described by the Internal Revenue Service, "liquidity is the ability to quickly convert property to cash or pay a liability. Said another way, liquidity is the ability to readily convert an asset, business, business ownership interest or security into cash without significant loss of principal. A Discount for Lack of Liquidity (DLOL) is an amount or percentage deducted from the value of an ownership interest to reflect the relative inability to quickly convert property to cash."[1]

Similarly, the lack of control needs to be taken into account. Lack of control refers to the fact that someone would pay less for an investment for which they don't have decision-making control. A minority investment by an outsider in a family business would not give that individual control over decision-making.

While restricting share ownership naturally lessens the value of shares—the smaller the market, the lower the price they may command—there are strategies to mitigate the downside of such a restriction. One of the most commonly used is an agreement wherein the company promises to create a market for anyone wishing to sell their shares—often, by the company buying back the shares itself. This boosts liquidity while helping ensure the orderly transfer of shares, which helps protect the ownership of the company.

Because family members who want to sell their shares will likely want the highest value possible, the topic of discounts is often contentious. On the flip side, family members who wish to gift their shares to succeeding generations will want a lower share valuation to decrease the value of their gift. This dichotomy presents families with an opportunity to develop very specific valuation methodologies for liquidity and ownership transitions.

Education is an important focus in the development of shareholder agreements. Helping owners understand how share valuations are conducted and why discounts are taken is very important. And, clearly spelling out the valuation methodology to be used is a critical component of any shareholder agreement. Finally, as we mentioned earlier, getting a shareholder agreement in place while the ownership group is small is very helpful. In our experience, it is extremely unlikely that a large ownership group will gain unanimous approval for an agreement. Moreover, if even one owner doesn't sign the agreement, it loses value for the rest because it is only binding for those who sign.

Owners' Roles and Responsibilities

When considering who gets to own what, it can be helpful to first think about your definition of the role, rights, and responsibilities of owners. In effect, what does it mean to be an owner? What skills and knowledge must you have, regardless of your career choice? No matter whether you are a chef or a forest ranger, what does every owner need to be capable of doing?

One way to start defining these guidelines is to approach them as you would leadership succession. In that situation, you would establish the attributes and abilities required for particular roles. From there, you would identify people capable of meeting those requirements.

You can do a similar sort of exercise with ownership. Imagine what optimal ownership looks like for the future of the business. What type of owners will reflect the values that guide decision-making in the business, and will those owners be supportive of decisions made by management? In some cases, family members, if given the choice, would rather not become shareholders of the business. However, they might not share that with senior-generation members for fear of looking ungrateful.

Below is a set of guidelines that family members may find helpful when making the difficult decisions associated with ownership continuity.

Owners are entitled to the following:

- the right to vote on the directors nominated by the board;
- the right to nominate directors and propose shareholder resolutions;
- the right to sell their shares of stock (subject to any restrictions in company bylaws or a shareholder agreement);
- the right to dividends if they are declared by the corporation;
- the right to receive accurate and timely information concerning their investments;
- the right to voice their questions and concerns to the board and/or management;
- the right to vote on business matters concerning purchase or sale of major assets and change in the governance structure of the business (e.g., bylaws).

Owners have a responsibility to

- come to agreement as an ownership group on values, vision, and goals that will guide the business and communicate these clearly to management and the board;
- clarify philosophy and expectations for issues at the intersection of family and business (e.g., family employment, financial expectations, code of conduct, family role in leadership);
- ensure excellent governance, not only in their choice of directors but also in establishing a mechanism through which family ownership matters can be discussed and resolved;
- work as partners with management and the board, endorsing and supporting strategy and monitoring the business to assure it reflects the values, vision, and goals the owners have set forth;

- educate themselves on the business so that they can make informed ownership decisions;
- represent the company well when participating in activities where they are recognized as owners;
- respect the chain of command, speaking to the board or senior management about issues of concern, and allowing management to do their job;
- proactively manage individual wealth and its transfer across generations so that personal final decisions do not put the overall ownership group in peril;
- understand the ownership structure of their business, including trusts and shareholder agreements.

Communication of these rights and responsibilities to younger generations can help them understand the importance of the role and what the elder generation will expect of them. By the same token, if the elder generation finds they have genuine concern about the ability of subsequent generations to meet the challenges of ownership, selling the business may become a more viable option. Finally, the rights and responsibilities document creates a template for ownership education.

The Importance of Education

Don't make the mistake of assuming that younger family members somehow will gain the knowledge and experience needed to take on the responsibilities of ownership, as though the process can occur through osmosis. Rather, organized education is a pivotal step in helping ensure that subsequent generations of owners know what is expected of them as owners and are prepared to meet those obligations. That further strengthens ownership continuity.

Education can start at a very early age. For instance, some owners take young children to the grocery store to show them the value and function of money. (Of course, this has become more abstract in an age in which everything is paid for with a credit or debit card!) Children at a young age become educated about family values around the dinner table. If you meet as a large group, cousins can participate in an educational session about the products or services offered by the business (even at a young age children are curious about such things). Parents may give children small amounts of money, which the kids may subsequently donate to an animal shelter or other charity. In fact, cousins could do this together. It is a great opportunity for them to learn about individual styles, compromise, and collaboration. These and other strategies implant the seed early on of what it means to be an owner and the varied responsibilities and opportunities ownership can afford them.

Education programs can vary considerably from one family to another. With some, it's a rather informal process. For others, it's a highly detailed, comprehensive arrangement with a systematic progression from one activity and program to another. Some families place an emphasis on making the learning process as much fun as possible for younger family members. At the Hussey Seating Company, a sixth-generation seating manufacturer in North Berwick, Maine, younger family members who attend the annual family forum learn about the company business through a scavenger hunt and trivia contests. In the Middleton family (introduced in Chapter 1), children enjoy tours of the factories where baby clothes are manufactured. They have opportunities to observe various activities required to produce a garment, from fabric laying to cutting, sewing, and packaging. Any of the next-generation activities can be tailored in an age-appropriate way. We work with families who start the education process even at toddler age (the most successful education programs are the ones that are most fun, particularly at early ages)!

One of the challenges that many families face, particularly when younger children are involved, is beginning the process of ownership education without going into financial specifics. Some parents may worry that, if younger family members know how much the business is worth or how wealthy the family is, it might lead to rash or ill-considered decisions. The simple solution is to address ownership education and continuity without necessarily putting a dollar figure on the discussion. After all, the topics of ownership of shares, philanthropy, and community involvement can be thoroughly discussed outside the framework of the money involved. Those numbers can enter the conversation when you decide the timing is appropriate.

Building the Ownership Team

One of the values of early ownership education is that it presents the opportunity to begin to develop an ownership team at an early age. Whether or not owners work in the business, they will be required to make important decisions together. Should we keep the business or sell it? Are we comfortable taking on our first nonfamily CEO? What should we do about an owner who is being disruptive? What if some owners want partial or full liquidity? The list could go on.

In the second generation, the ownership group consists of siblings, who most often have grown up in the same household with a similar education on the expectations of ownership. Once a family business reaches the cousin generation or beyond, new owners often have a very different level of understanding of ownership and its obligations. And, because they haven't grown up together, they haven't had the opportunity to work together to make important decisions. Understanding that one cousin is quick to make a decision, but may come back later and change their mind, while another is quiet while they think through their options but are decisive in the end is important information.

Building trust in one another is commensurate to tackling tough issues. Finally, while the leader of a business is recognized as such and respected for the authority of their position, there is not always a natural leader of the ownership group. So, the ability to work together and achieve consensus without this natural leader becomes even more important.

In later-stage businesses, it is imperative that the elder generation thinks through the implications of their decisions for the who, how, and when of ownership transition with respect to how they will affect the ability to develop a solid leadership team. Often, this exercise of thinking through the team dynamics will lead the current owners to see the value of coordinated ownership transition planning.

The Importance of Coordinated Ownership Transition Planning

Ideally, ownership continuity planning across the family would occur in perfect harmony. Everyone would agree on how to transfer shares, when to transfer them, to whom to transfer them, and the optimal time for this to take place, and would communicate these decisions to the members of their generation.

Not surprisingly, the opposite occurs more often. For instance, one family member decides to divide his shares equally among all his children; another chooses just one child for her shares. Some family members begin gifting shares to relatively young family members, while another feels it important that subsequent generations mature and gain experience in the business before receiving shares. Still others may gift the shares but place them in a trust where the beneficiary has limited access and decision-making authority.

Diverse ownership transfer scenarios within the family can have serious consequences. For instance, let's assume the head of one branch of a family has done a terrific job of mapping out the particulars of her ownership continuity strategy, and in so doing, has passed along shares to her children with the utmost tax efficiency. Her brother, on the other hand, has let the issue slide completely. He suffers a heart attack, dies, and the shares pass to his children, who lack the funds to pay the necessary estate taxes. In the end, the business—including that portion owned by the responsible family member—has to be sold to meet the estate tax obligation. In effect, the one person who did everything right suffers because her sibling didn't take the time to develop an estate plan.

This makes coordinated ownership planning essential to avoid both financial and emotional problems. That doesn't necessarily mean everyone must do the same thing. What is important is that family members get together to let each other know what they are doing with regard to ownership succession, or at least to let others know about what has been put in place to manage a sudden death. Although talking about these sorts of issues can be awkward and occasionally contentious, it is very helpful if family members share what they're doing, even if it is with a smaller group (such as the board or trustees). It can help boost family harmony—the feeling of coming together as a group to help ensure the stability of the family and the business. Moreover, if some family members are ignoring the issue entirely or are taking steps that are counter to the security of the family and the business, others can take the opportunity to protect themselves and their share of ownership as much as possible.

Other Issues to Consider

Ownership continuity requires a significant investment of time, detailed discussions, and careful decisions. While we have addressed a number of critical issues in detail, we have only touched on the technical complexities of how shares may be held. In the effort to minimize estate taxes as well as to provide for the orderly transition of shares, many families consider passing their shares through special vehicles, including trusts, voting trusts, and family limited partnerships, among others.

It is not the goal of this book to address the pros and cons of these strategies. However, it is important for families to be aware of all of their options. We strongly recommend working with a team of advisers, including estate planners, accountants, lawyers, financial advisers, and any other trusted advisers to the family, to ensure you have identified the best options.

However valuable these strategies may prove to be for certain businesses in certain types of situations, approach them prudently. Before putting anything into place, ask your advisers whether and how any of these steps can be undone. How long do they typically remain in place? Are there any consequences or aftereffects that you overlooked that are it is essential that you be aware of?

Then, take what you know and project yourself into your children and grandchildren's shoes. Imagine every possibility of how these decisions might affect them. Will a particular decision made today ensure their continued security, or will it drive some of them away from the business completely? Looked at another way, even if the immediate impact is highly beneficial—such as a significant tax saving—think about the long-term ramifications. Will a hefty tax saving now be worth a long-festering problem 25 or even 50 years down the line?

How to Begin the Ownership Continuity Process

As is the case with other far-reaching issues, such as developing vision and values statements, it is important to make ownership continuity a priority to which a family devotes ample time and energy. Schedule meetings during off-hours and earmark sufficient time to agree on basic principles and concepts. It's a very personal undertaking and should be approached in that vein.

It is also critical to view the issue of ownership in terms of continuity rather than succession. Succession connotes the end of an era, a departure. Continuity, on the other hand, suggests endurance and a passing of the torch. Continuity will affect generations to come, not just the next person down the line.

While these points may mirror those that apply to the development of vision and values, it's best to approach the nuts and bolts of ownership continuity in a different manner. Rather than involving most or all family members from the outset, it's more efficient to begin with just the current owners. We recommend scheduling meetings with current owners to begin discussing ownership priorities, obligations, specifics of ownership continuity, shareholder agreements, and a time frame for implementation.

Limiting input at the beginning of the process allows for current owners to focus on those issues and goals that are of greatest value to them. After all, even though they're planning when and how to pass along ownership of the business to others, they are still in charge and, as such, have the responsibility and obligation to map out plans that they feel will work best for the group as a whole. Then, once those issues and plans have been addressed, the information can be presented to the next generation for their consideration and feedback.

There are two final issues to bear in mind. As we mentioned earlier, it's often not possible to draw up a plan for ownership continuity that's completely consistent with the needs of all family groups and members. For instance, some families may be a blend of bloodline and adopted children, with the addition of new family members making coordinated planning difficult. In other family members, longstanding riffs or feuds can make planning or even the simple act of communication impossible.

One way to approach these challenging circumstances is to use an intermediary. That could be a trusted family adviser whose objectivity is unquestioned. A parent, aunt, or uncle can also serve to bring distant parties closer together.

If that is not feasible, it is important to plan with the interests of your particular segment of the family foremost in mind. As we cited in an earlier example, even the most prepared family group's future can be compromised by another whose planning is shoddy, outdated, or nonexistent. If you can't seem to come together, make sure to protect yourself and those closest to you to the best of your ability.

Additionally, don't lose sight of your family vision and values when considering ownership continuity. Like other elements of your family and business, those can form a reliable bedrock from which to map out effective decisions and long-term planning.

Last, we encourage you to be aware of the importance of ownership continuity planning in conjunction with appropriate estate planning. The two activities are too inter-related to approach them as wholly separate entities. There are several behaviors or beliefs that can get in the way of continuity planning. We most often see four behaviors:

- Procrastination. Far too many people put off estate planning in deference to what they deem to be more immediate concerns. Don't be one of those people. Moreover, keep your plan as up to date as possible. Related to procrastination is the owner's hope, often despite evidence to the contrary, that the next generation will become more interested, more committed, competent, or passionate about the business. That may happen, or it may never happen. It is not a valid reason to put off continuity planning (which evolves over time anyway).
- Confusing equality with fairness. Different family members have likely made differing contributions to your business. In addition, next-generation family members have different individual needs. There is fairness in responding to those distinctions, but that doesn't necessarily mean that everyone should receive the same thing (or even receive things of equal value). Equal doesn't mean fair—and often "unequal" represents the fairest allocation or reward decisions you will make.
- Failing to seek competent advice. There are many credible sources of expertise. You should make careful and thoughtful choices about whom to include in your ownership transfer and estate planning process. We often see owners engaging their long-time legal or tax advisers because they trust them. That makes sense from a trust perspective, but you also need to ensure that they possess the experience and expertise that are specific to these particular subjects. Advisers are "specialists" for good reason.
- Failing to discuss with your family the details and rationale for specific estate decisions. People don't like to be surprised at the best of times. When they are mourning your absence, surprise can actually result in many of

the emotions that you hope to avoid: anger, resentment, betrayal, or rejection. As difficult as it can be to communicate these plans to family members while you're living, it's always worse to have an "outsider" share those very personal and important decisions with your children. Optimally, you want your beneficiaries to learn of your decisions from you.

Planning for ownership transitions and other estate decisions requires thoughtful and sometimes painstaking deliberations. Sharing your ideas with next-generation family members takes courage, and is not without emotion. Yet it is an investment of time that will reap the intrinsic rewards that will serve to sustain family relationships, the business, and your legacy after you are gone.

In Brief

- Families need to take a broad, comprehensive view of long-term ownership continuity. This view includes looking far into the future to model the potential implications of ownership transition decisions.
- How ownership will be transferred varies across families and across branches within one family. Communication among members of the ownership group is important in order to understand the implications of these variations.
- While technical advisers, in the areas of estate, tax and financial planning, are crucial to successful ownership continuity, don't let financial issues override family vision and values.
- It is important that owners understand precisely what ownership means and what is involved. Good owners are those who were prepared for their roles through a thoughtful education process.

4

Leadership Continuity

Once you have developed the foundation for continuity by articulating your family vision and values and establishing clear parameters for ownership, the next step is to address leadership continuity. Without effective leadership, your business cannot survive and grow. Leadership continuity planning ensures you have the right team in place to secure the future of your business.

Your planning in this area will be informed by the vision and values you have established. Addressing issues such as what role you see the family playing in the business or how you treat family working in the business are crucial to the family's vision as well as leadership continuity planning. Moreover, ownership continuity planning goes hand in hand with leadership continuity. Overlapping questions include: Should only family members who are employed in the business own shares? Do you expect the next generation of employees to buy shares from the current generation? Will the timing of share transfer and leadership transfer be coordinated?

Setting the Context for Effective Leadership Now and in the Future

You have already taken the first steps in leadership continuity planning by defining your vision. Among other things, the vision addresses the role you hope the family will play in the business. Alignment of family expectations regarding who will lead the business is crucial to family harmony as well as business success. That said, there is no right answer. One of our clients has commented, "Without a Smith in the CEO seat, we might as well sell the business." Another asserts, "We find there is more family harmony if we have a nonfamily CEO. It reduces the likelihood of jockeying for position and hurt feelings when someone's son or daughter is not chosen." A third perspective: "We'd prefer a family CEO. But, if there is no one in the family who can run the business well, we won't sacrifice business results."

Regardless of your perspective on family leadership, leadership continuity planning is essential to ensure you have well-prepared leaders in place to guide the future of your family enterprise. So, once you've decided the role of family in family leadership, how do you define what type of leader you need?

Leadership needs are inextricably linked with the strategy of the business. Too often, leadership continuity planning starts by considering what leadership candidates are available instead of what the business requires. Yet, business success is dependent on the development and execution of a strategy that will help preserve and grow the business. And the strategic vision for the future of the business should impact your decision about future leadership.

Influences external to your business require your strategy to evolve. That evolution takes many forms, depending on the power and source of these influences. Some businesses operate in environments where strategic change can be incremental. In other circumstances, the force of change necessitates fundamental strategic shifts. Some of you may have faced this kind of pressure—requiring you to fundamentally reinvent your business or materially alter your products or services.

You might be in a business that has seen significant industry consolidation. Perhaps you find yourself serving markets that are shrinking or utilizing distribution channels that have consolidated. To take just one example, the downturn in US home building in the past several years has changed the long-term outlook for many industries who provide supplies for this industry. Given the nature and pace of change, be it technological change, globalization, or industry consolidation, many industries are stumbling toward extinction, or, at the very least, facing considerably slower growth.

Other industries are growing at a very rapid pace. Is your business involved in solar power or the environment, biotechnology, or 3-D print manufacturing? No matter your specific operation, technology alone has dramatically altered product life cycles, distribution channels, and supply-chain management. It has influenced the way customers consume products and services and, in so doing, helped shape the future trajectory of businesses of all sorts.

It's also important to bear in mind that the pace of change in industries has created a much more narrow margin for error. Even a seemingly minor misstep might provide the window of opportunity your competitors need. Now and even more so in the future, companies may not recover from a delayed reaction to market changes, poorly executed strategies or misguided leadership.

With those factors in mind, it's not just possible but also probable that the future leader of your business will need to bring to that position different skills, experiences, insights, and a depth of judgment and wisdom to help the family realize its vision for continuity. What worked in the past may be rather irrelevant or ineffective tomorrow. At the same time, the rapid rate of change creates opportunities for family businesses—with the flexibility of private ownership—to expand into new businesses that leverage their strengths and fundamentally reinvent themselves. Regardless of the opportunities or threats presented by the business environment, leadership transitions provide an opportunity to address the changing needs of the business in a way that serves the family for the long run.

Why Leadership Development is Critical—and Often Overlooked

It is difficult to imagine a set of family business owners who would say that having an effective business leader is not critical to their success. But, the fact is, many family businesses do not have a clear picture of the skills required for someone to successfully lead their business, not to mention a plan in place to ensure that their current and future leaders develop those required skills.

The reasons family businesses overlook the importance of a clear leadership profile vary. In some instances, a leader may simply assume that a son or daughter will eventually step into the leadership role. Therefore, the leadership profile is limited to the candidates available. Moreover, for the current leader, creating a leadership development program to prepare the next generation is a sobering reminder of mortality—the fact that "One day, I'm not going to be sitting in this chair." Or, the current leader may not want to address the fact that his or her skills and experience may be lacking in certain areas.

Similarly, family businesses often lack formal career and leadership development. This oversight may be rooted in a belief that steps taken to build skills and experience in a potential leader are a diversion from "real work" (manufacturing and selling a product or service, for instance) or the fact that many family business owners and leaders haven't had exposure to an effective leadership development process.[1]

Not only is a systematic plan necessary to identify potential candidates and prepare them accordingly, but it's also important because leadership cannot function in a vacuum. Someday you will have to find a new person to occupy the top chair and she is going to need support of a strong team. When planning for the next generation of leadership, it's important to consider the full leadership team. A successful leader is strengthened by an infrastructure that develops competence across the management team and creates a culture that nurtures and supports decision-makers.

Leadership and career development programs effectively serve two masters. One is the individual who is looking to further her career. The other is the business, which will require fully developed and competent leadership in the future. Thus, a solid leadership continuity plan will serve the business directly as well as the individuals who benefit from the investment in their careers. Moreover, leadership development is not a discrete task, with a beginning and an end. To ensure leadership continuity, qualified leaders needs to be constantly nurtured.

Step One in Leadership Continuity Planning:
Defining Leadership Needs

To help diffuse the challenges associated with selecting a leader—particularly when candidates are family members—the best starting point for the discussion of leadership needs is what the business will, or could, look like in the future. It can be valuable to begin the discussion with four salient questions that are bound to branch out into a variety of subsequent issues:

- What will make the business successful in the future?
- What needs to be changed in order to accomplish that objective?
- What skills, experiences, and attributes must one possess in order to be an optimal future leader?
- Who has the best talents and abilities and development potential to lead the company toward that goal of success?[2]

These benchmark questions set the stage for a broad discussion. What is the landscape of our business now, and what will it look like in the future? Does the anticipated environment present opportunities to grow in new directions that leverage our strengths? What needs to be adjusted to account for expected changes in the environment? Do we have legacy businesses that have become unprofitable, but remain emotional assets? Can we improve their viability, or do we need to let them go?

From there, the discussion naturally segues into consideration of what skill sets and experience are required in the leader who will meet those challenges. This discussion will touch on some sensitive and critical issues:

- What if we have a vision of family leadership, but do not have a family member with the experience required to be successful in the anticipated business environment? What if they have a relevant experience, but lack the personal attributes required to champion successful growth in the business? Would we be willing to consider a nonfamily leader for a period of time, until we can prepare someone in the family? Is there someone within our organization who would be not only a good leader but also a good mentor for the next generation?

- What if the changing industry environment suggests a need for skills and experience that are not present in our top ranks? Would our organization accept a leader from the outside? How could we best help someone from the outside to understand our culture so as to increase their likelihood of success? And, how can we ensure that we don't have a gap in leadership the next time?
- If the skills and experience required seem difficult to find in a single person, would we consider a team model of leadership, encompassing multiple family members or family and nonfamily together? Can the job be divided into discrete pieces that allow each person to take charge as well as collaborate with others to get the job done?

While these challenging issues can be delicate or emotional for a family to consider, they are crucial to the success of the business. Rather than avoid them in hopes of skirting family conflict, it is better to return to the family vision and the foundation it provides. If the family has stated that its goal is to be in business together for generations to come, then finding the leader most likely to guarantee that vision should be in the best interests of the family. If the family vision says that family leadership of the business is crucial, then the family may need to be willing to sacrifice business performance or to pay more to bring in a team to support the family leader.

As you begin to draw up the qualifications you feel will be appropriate for future leadership, it is helpful to bear in mind the tendency to find gravitate towards what we know and have experienced. This tendency can lead to development of a leadership profile similar to what you have today. If, your initial group discussion regarding the future of your business has led you to determine that there will likely be significant shifts in your market, competition, or even the very function of your business itself, then the leadership model of the past is not likely to apply.

Even if the business environment is stable, the business has likely grown and become more complex in the past decade or two. So, the leadership required in the past generation is typically not the same as what is required in this generation. In a recent discussion with an ownership group about next-generation leadership, one owner in her sixties asserted that she didn't feel a college degree should be mandatory for the CEO position because her father didn't have one when he led the company. Her cousins quickly pushed back, reminding her that the environment had changed fundamentally since her father ran the business—a business that was now four times larger!

Another way to gauge whether you need to focus on leadership candidates with significantly different skills and experience is to examine your own feelings about the business. It may be surprising, but a number of family business owners have told us that the exponential growth and increased complexity of their business have sometimes left them overwhelmed and feeling that they are not optimally equipped to provide effective and successful leadership themselves.

This suggests the need to look to leadership successors with a very different array of skills and strengths, and it offers a compelling argument for a well-thought-out and comprehensive training and development program. No leader wants their successor to fail, and this is particularly so with their children and other family members. They want to create circumstances that will provide for success for their future leaders.

Who Defines Leadership Needs?

The task of developing the future leadership profile is a challenging one. Unlike the ownership continuity discussions, where current owners have the authority and responsibility to determine the future, the task of defining leadership needs typically rests within the business domain. While the family can provide direction on the importance it places on family leadership, the family is ill-suited to define leadership needs. First and foremost, the family may not have the knowledge required to define the leadership profile. Equally important, the family will have significant conflicts of interest in determining leadership needs, as their evaluation will biased by their feelings about family candidates.

So, current business leadership needs to rely on the input of the existing leadership team as well as advisers will solid knowledge of business needs and capabilities of internal talent. If you have a board of directors, they should always be included in planning for leadership transition at the senior management level. Board members typically provide great insights on leadership. They are also a source of objectivity, which in this process becomes very important.

If you do not have a formal board with independent advisers or directors, you may belong to an organization (Young President's Organization or Vistage, for example) or a trade association that can provide valuable counsel on leadership transition. In addition, you may have trusted advisers (such as lawyers, accountants, or bankers)who have become familiar with key players in the business and the family. They can share their thinking on important considerations as you move through the process.

Senior managers often provide valuable input on leadership options as well, particularly since they have intimate knowledge of the industry as well as impending opportunities and pitfalls. Keep in mind, however, that their views may be biased by their personal desires to attain a more senior position as well as their feelings about other candidates in the organization.

If you are fortunate to have a strong head of human resources, that person could also provide crucial insight into the conversation.

A rigorous annual performance evaluation process is a valuable tool in the leadership selection process. Results of the performance evaluation process of existing senior management can enlighten the conversation on desired leadership skills and experience as well. Examining the current management team's strengths and gaps can help you think about which skills you desire that are already present and which are missing. If you do not have a good performance evaluation process in place, the leadership succession planning process can be a motivator to develop one.

Some family members (and nonfamily management) attend outside courses and conferences on leadership in an effort to strengthen their skills and prepare for leadership transition. Many of these educational venues offer assessment tools that will enhance your understanding of your key leadership traits, strengths, and weaknesses. One organization that business-owning families have used with consistent success is the Center for Creative Leadership. In addition, 360 degree feedback processes are very insightful for emerging next generation leaders.

A next-generation member of the Middleton family mentioned earlier shared his experience in a family meeting that focused on the future leadership of the business: "My parents used to force me to come to these meetings all through high school, and I resented it. But now that I'm in college, I can really appreciate the time that's invested in these decisions—it's awesome that I am included, and I'm grateful to be invited now."

The conversation about the skills and experience required to successfully guide your organization is a critical one. A successful outcome often depends on collaborative discussions with all of the groups mentioned above, as well as from careful personal reflection by the individual or individuals currently in charge.

Steps to a Leadership Development Program

Once you have a sense of the profile of the leader your business will require in the future, you need to give careful thought to how a leadership development program can be managed successfully. As you will see, this can prove to be an intense but exciting period.

First, it's important to take stock of where a potential leader is in their development. Consider what skills they have now, what skills the leader still needs to acquire and develop, a strategy to help obtain those skills, and a way to gauge the leader's overall progress. These parameters will be based on those skills and experience you've determined your business will likely require in the future.

Attitude is a key component of this development. Embarking on a leadership development programs requires potential successors to be self-aware, take initiative, bring energy and passion to the journey, and energize those associated with the successor's development.

It is important for the candidate to have a hand in creating their own leadership development plan. While a mentor and others are valuable in developing the plan, the potential successor should be sufficiently introspective and candid in assessing their personal and professional skills, what they need to nurture, and the most effective way to help realize the established goals.

The leadership development path will vary based on the business. One strategy emphasizes that the candidate be involved in areas that are critical to the business, including gaining responsibility for profit and loss, breathing new life into a struggling component of the business, addressing delicate personnel issues, or taking on relationship challenges with customers, vendors or other stakeholders. Other examples include a discrete project, such as overseeing a divestiture or acquisition, managing complex financial decisions, or successfully negotiating a union contract.

From a practical standpoint, leadership development can happen in a number of ways. One effective strategy places leadership candidates in a variety of positions and responsibilities over time, such as sales, marketing, strategic planning, and other duties. While candidates gain experience in a number of positions within the company, management can also get a sense of their leadership capabilities and ability to understand how the overall company operates. Another benefit of this approach is that it helps build confidence among leadership candidates. They are acquiring experience in running an aspect of the business in which success and growth are readily identifiable.

Another approach is the use of what might be referred to as "stretch assignments." Leadership candidates are called upon to take on increasingly challenging or ambitious projects, such as a new division of the company or a completely new product line. Of course, the nature of this sort of approach will depend on the specifics of your business. But the idea is to encourage candidates to challenge themselves and assume tasks that are increasingly demanding.

In smaller organizations, the variety of roles or projects required to expand leadership responsibility may not be available. Take the example of one client who hired us to help prepare a second-generation successor to his father. His father was in charge, and the client was second in command. There were no other jobs the successor could take. The key was to provide him with exposure to all the roles and responsibilities of his father. Some were day to day, such as dealing with escalated customer complaints. Others were less frequent, such as meeting with bankers to review loan covenants.

In this case, we put together a list of all the responsibilities his father had carried out and developed a time frame in which they could be gradually transitioned to the son. There was a plan for the transition of each responsibility that included exposure to the responsibility as well as communication within the organization about the change. In the case of external responsibilities, such as dealing with insurance and bankers, his father took him to several meetings with these business partners before he took over the responsibility on his own. (See appendices for a detailed leadership development plan)A benefit to the crescendo of increasing responsibility in all of these options is that it is very much hands on. It encourages vision, creative thought, and problem-solving skills. It is a form of leadership instruction that is entirely experiential; it cannot be taught in a classroom.

Of course, that form of learning comes with a risk of missteps or outright failure. But that, too, is a valuable form of instruction. Senior-generation family members know better than anyone that everyone makes mistakes. What is important for the next-generation successors is that they understand that mistakes are acceptable and are merely another type of learning experience.

The Importance of Starting Early

It goes without saying that planning and implementing a successful leadership continuity strategy take time. In essence, developing leaders is an ongoing process in the organization. Moreover, leadership development is important throughout the business. It is not just the CEO leadership role that merits development attention but all leadership positions in the business.

With regard to family members, it is helpful to begin to lay the foundation for leadership when children are young. We encourage you to help your young children understand the importance of values and, as it becomes appropriate, to also educate and expose them to decision-making processes in the business, including employee development, financial management, stakeholder relationships, and other leadership responsibilities. For instance, if you come home from work with a valuable story to tell, take the time to share it with your children. A story about how you got two very different people to work together effectively can imbue your children with a valuable lesson at an early age.

By the same token, don't make the mistake of going overboard by complaining about every problem or slip-up you experience in the business. That's not to say your portrayal to your children should be through rose-colored glasses; rather, strike a balance that captures both the rewards of the business as well as its challenges. One next-generation family member shares that she "didn't want the hassle of working in the business because of all the tension that my dad and uncle have had—it's just not worth it."

Two other points are worth mentioning. Don't convey the message to your children that a leadership role (or any role, for that matter) is an ironclad obligation. Instead, frame it as a potential opportunity they may wish to consider. By the same token, don't give them the idea that their roles as leaders are a fait accompli. Not only will they have to possess the skills and attributes that you have determined your business will need in the future, they will also have to earn their stripes.

Address Necessary Skills

The skill sets of the current leader are a component that needs to be addressed as well. Before you think about how you might develop the next generation of leaders, ask yourself the following question if you are currently in a leadership position: What do I need to work on so that I can help them develop? It may seem like an odd question, but self-reflection becomes critical to helping groom the next leader successfully. Might you need to communicate more clearly or offer more encouragement and reinforcement as your future successors go through the process? Are you demonstrating enough flexibility regarding the acceptance of potential successors' ideas, despite the fact that they are very different from your own? Are you open-minded enough to recognize and accept the fact that next-generation leaders might want a different work-life balance than what you've had? Is it OK that your son's approach to managing people is starkly different from yours? Is your daughter's willingness to take on more measured risk as a leader acceptable to you? Can you ask your children what they see as your greatest strengths and weaknesses as a leader? Prepare yourself for some surprises and, hopefully, some candor!

The Importance of Development

Following are some recommendations on important components of leadership development. While there is no iron clad rule concerning the value of these recommendations for all businesses, based on our experience the following are strong contributors to success:

- **Work outside the business.** Many companies urge family members in their twenties to begin their careers by working for several years for another company with no connection to the family business. This is an important developmental step for a number of reasons. First, a young person working for an outside company has to stand on their own two feet. In a work setting with no connection to the family, a last name likely means nothing in terms of how their work performance is judged. Not only can that bolster confidence and help develop new skills, it also gives the young person a fresh perspective on the family business and whether, in fact, they want to come on board or strike out on a professional path elsewhere. In addition, if they have been able to demonstrate success elsewhere, it creates credibility for that family member among management—this provides enormous value and further bolsters self-confidence for the family member.

  At Hamilton Shirts, Houston's oldest family-owned business, siblings David and Kelly Hamilton both worked elsewhere—David in investment banking and Kelly as a fundraiser for the Houston Ballet—before joining the family business. Kelly is quick to credit her father, Jim, for not pressuring the two of them to come on board immediately: "He always made it known that we were welcome, but that it wasn't something that we had to do. If we wanted to be rodeo clowns, we were free to be rodeo clowns."

- **Hire based on a job opening and suitable qualifications.** Once a family member has completed a period of outside employment, they should only be brought into the company when there's a job opening for which they are qualified. Not only can that allay concerns from nonfamily employees that a position was "created" for the family member, it reinforces the value that the hiring decision was made based on merit, not name. Here, you may already have a family employment policy in place that lays out basic requirements about education, work experience, the hiring process, and performance evaluations. Some companies don't mandate outside employment, but do have policies in place that make merit a clear requirement for advancement. For instance, in the White Castle chain of burger restaurants, family work parameters make it clear that everyone starts with the company by taking hamburger orders.

- **Ensure alignment between the position and the person.** Some potential successors start out at a relatively high level in the company. Others are better suited to starting at a much lower position. There are pluses and minuses to both. If, for instance, a succession candidate comes into the business at a position of some responsibility, they can quickly gain valuable experience in decision-making and other tasks. On the other hand, starting in a position of much lower import can help teach potential successors about all areas of the business, not just those more related to higher leadership positions. Regardless of the point of entry, family members should start working in positions that are commensurate with the skills and experience they bring to the job.

- **Make no guarantees.** Wherever you may choose to place a successor, it is important that they know from the start that their ascension to leadership is by no means guaranteed. It is a possibility, not a promise, depending how they meet a variety of criteria and steps. Moreover, every potential successor should have a clear vision of just what they will need to achieve to eventually assume a leadership capacity.

The Value of Mentors and Other Guides

While a candidate will be working with management in their leadership development, it is often helpful to engage in a relationship with one individual who is a "go-to" person for a variety of inquiries. Working with a mentor for several years or more can be an essential element of successful leadership development.

In essence, a mentor should help a developing young leader learn to exercise judgment, take calculated risks, embrace the value of transparency, and interact with others with understanding and empathy. Depending on the nature of the relationship and the experience of a particular mentor, they can also address specific professional skills.

An ideal mentor may be a trusted adviser or someone outside of the company who nonetheless knows the business well and can help guide their younger colleague. For instance, if the mentor works for another company, they can have the candidate visit their business to gain a fresh perspective on another organization's functions, policies, and practices.

Whoever you may consider to be a suitable mentor, they should not be the successor's parent or boss. Given the nature of those sorts of relationships, a candidate may be cautious about raising volatile issues or other delicate matters. An outsider is much better suited to address those sorts of situations.

The mentoring relationship can take on both formal and informal aspects. While a mentor can help a candidate chart their progress and growth in meeting developmental benchmarks, the mentor can also serve as an informal sounding board and source of feedback. Sometimes, a relaxed chat over a cup of coffee can be every bit as meaningful as the most structured review session.

Board members can also prove to be valuable guides, if. your business has a board of directors. A director can be asked to help oversee leadership development criteria and monitor candidates' progress. A director's perspective can be particularly insightful. For example, if a director feels that a candidate is being insufficiently challenged—a common circumstance for a parent who doesn't want their child to fail— the director can intervene to suggest that the candidate take on greater responsibilities or more demanding assignments.

Another useful experience is for a leadership candidate to serve on an outside boards of directors. That can be difficult to find with regard to corporate boards, but nonprofit boards provide great opportunities to teach not only leadership attributes but also to strengthen team building and collaboration skills, and the importance of compromise.

Winning Legitimacy and Authority

While the path to developing professional skills and exposure to business practices is fairly clear, developing a leader's capacity to earn the confidence and respect of others is more complicated.

Many of the steps previously outlined—working for another company, taking on a number of different roles in your business, and an increasing record of responsibility and success, among others—can be critical in helping a potential leader win the respect and trust of those with whom they work. That can be true for any leadership candidate, but particularly so for a family member who, in their own way, has to prove all the more that an eventual leadership role isn't just the result of having a particular last name.

Credibility isn't about who you are—you cannot inherit or be anointed with it—it can only be earned over time. It's about others' perceptions of what successor candidates bring to the company. You may know that your son or daughter is completely equipped to be the next leader; others may not. You need to manage and develop the perception of others because that can set the stage for the potential successor's winning respect and trust. It creates the foundation for acceptance, loyalty, commitment, energy, and other factors that help cement business continuity.

How long does that take? It depends, but a general rule of thumb is several years. The time period can be shortened if the successor performs particularly well in their development, such as helping introduce a valuable new product or service or beginning a completely new venture. Also helpful is having the candidate occupy a variety of roles in the business, especially if they start at a relatively low level and successfully works their way up. Naturally, the time required to develop next-generation leaders varies with what they bring to the job in the first place. If your daughter has an MBA and has worked elsewhere in a leadership role, her developmental arc will likely look different than that of your son who was a language major in college and worked for a few years in an unrelated field such as teaching or journalism.

The Murugappa Group (mentioned in Chapter 2) incorporated a variety of approaches to leadership development. One fourth-generation member worked for two years at GE Capital in India. The remaining members of this generation accumulated work experience within the family business itself, holding positions of escalating responsibility as they grew older.

A strategy that's best avoided is creating a completely new position for the leadership candidate. That can be particularly damaging to a family member, as it may strike other employees as unduly accommodating. The only instance when such an option should be considered is when the needs of the business mandate it, and when the "bench strength" in your business can support that kind of significant leadership change.

The Length of the Process

Ideally, leadership continuity planning—like other continuity strategies—should be a lifelong process that's never neglected for very long.

In our experience, it really takes at least five years—and often more—to groom the next generation of leaders. In fact, we've worked with companies in which it's taken as long as 15 years to plan and successfully execute a leadership development program. Take, for example, a client with three brothers in the second generation, all in their early fifties, who operate a large manufacturing business. In an ownership meeting, they developed a vision for the company that focuses on the importance of strong leadership, regardless of whether it is family or nonfamily. The crucial component, they feel, is that the leader come from within the organization.

While the three of them took over directly from their father, their children are much younger. So, if one child is interested in leading, they will still be too young when the respective father or uncle hits a mandatory retirement age of 70. Therefore, even in their fifties, with close to 20 years still available to them, these brothers are already thinking about whom in the organization they can groom to step into a leadership position. They know that they should be preparing this individual, or a set of individuals, now, so that they will be comfortable stepping down and leaving the organization when the time comes.

Keeping a visual timeline of the career path of your senior managers and their likely time to retirement is a good tool to support leadership continuity planning. Refer to the appendix for a visual timeline of this process.

The more time you have, the better positioned you are to leverage every development opportunity, from allowing candidates sufficient time to gain experience in a broad array of positions within the company to enlisting the assistance and guidance of mentors, board members, and others. And know that you may start down one road and have to shift course. Your child may change her mind and decide the family business isn't for her (by the same token, some children may wish to avoid the family business completely in early adulthood, only to develop an interest later in life). Your son may prove himself a competent manager, but not demonstrate the skills and attributes that a visionary needs to bring to the leadership position. That by itself can threaten continuity of the business.

How long the process can take will also depend on how many candidates are in the mix. In some cases, a business will designate a member of the next generation as the successor of choice and work closely with that one person—an option that carries some significant caveats, among them a lack of interest or ability in the designated successor.

Leadership continuity planning is a never-ending process. The ideal goal is to look at all of your employees who possess growth potential and think about what you need to be doing to take them to the next level, be they family or nonfamily. Certainly, these efforts become more intense and focused when you know that a key leadership position will be vacant in the next few years. However, it is a good practice to develop people regardless of where they may move. It sends a signal that you are willing to invest in them but also that you have high expectations that they will need to live up to. For smaller organizations, there may not always be a new position with a new title to which each employee can aspire. But there are always opportunities to expand employees' skill sets by exposing them to new responsibilities.

The Importance of Transparency

Throughout the entire process of leadership development, it is essential that family as well as nonfamily members be kept apprised of progress and changes in the overall program. While feedback on the process is important, feedback on candidate performance should not be shared outside of the leadership team. Family members need to feel that the process is appropriate, but do not need to be privy to the challenges faced by next-generation leaders as they may bias their perspective on the future leader.

A lack of communication, or a perception of secrecy around leadership transitions, will often create flight risks among your senior people. Moreover, in the absence of communication, actions can be misinterpreted. If one candidate attends a conference or is enrolled in an executive education program, this action may be construed as evidence that they have been chosen as the leader. It is important to think through how assignments or perks given to candidates may be perceived by the rest of the organization.

Consistent communication and a transparent process are critical to the end result of any leadership succession decision. If it's made evident to everyone that a designated successor candidate was chosen fairly, even those who may disagree with the choice will likely feel more comfortable with the decision. Additionally, if it's made clear that the choice was based on rigorous criteria and subsequent development, the chosen candidate will likely assume the leadership role smoothly and have a head start on earning the respect and confidence of others. However, if a lack of communication hints that a family member was chosen because they were the family favorite or didn't have to meet any sort of requisite qualifications, a rocky transition is likely to follow—including a possible exodus of nonfamily management.

The decision as to who will take on the role of leadership in a company should be delivered not only with supporting information as to why that decision was made but should also take place with empathy for any other candidates who were not selected. For candidates not chosen, there may be other opportunities that are created for them in order to avoid losing them.

While important, communication should be carefully planned, with consideration to how these news will be interpreted by stakeholders within the family and management. We recently worked with a company in which a woman had served as CEO for ten years. Out of the blue, management sprung the news that they had named her successor and that she should step down. Needless to say, that left some hard feelings. A consistent and transparent form of communication could have made the entire process far less jolting.

Styles of Leadership Transition

There are five common ways for a leadership transfer to occur. Some are clearly more effective than others.

1. Cold Turkey

The leader retains control until they die, suffer an accident or illness, or cannot continue for some other reason. The successor then assumes control immediately.

- **Advantages**—Succession does take place, and, however abrupt, it spares the family and the business the strain and tension that can often characterize longer, drawn-out transitions.
- **Drawbacks**—Successors who are suddenly thrust into a leadership role have little time to prepare. In addition, there may be no obvious successor, so conflict around that decision ensues. If the successor is young and inexperienced, and there is no board in place, it is likely going to be very difficult for them to gain the credibility they will need to lead the business successfully.

2. Delay and Delay and…

Despite repeated promises to implement some sort of transition, a leader maintains control.

- **Advantages**—If a strong leader is in place, they continue to run the organization well.
- **Drawbacks**—There are several significant drawbacks. First, the designated successor may get frustrated and leave the company. Additionally, if the delay drags on long enough, the successor may actually retire, leaving the business without a successor. Last, the leader's hesitancy to pass along control may also prompt an unwillingness to pursue opportunities that have even a modest amount of risk. Hesitancy in one area can carry over to other areas. Perhaps the most important drawback is that the successor doesn't get a chance at leadership and becomes emotionally disengaged from the business.

3. Here, Gone, Here, Gone

The leader passes control along very quickly, then drops from sight for a while, only to reappear and reassume control.

- **Advantages**—However briefly, succession does take place, allowing the new leader to gain some experience.

- **Drawbacks**—Like the delay scenario, the successor may become frustrated and leave the business. The reappearance of the retired leader sends a number of messages (none of them good) to others in the business, which in turn shapes their perceptions of the successor. Most important, the business will suffer from a lack of sustained, consistent direction. The management team will not know who to turn to for a decision, and may be forced to side with the retiring leader or his successor.

4. Gradual/Progressive

The leader gradually passes along more and more control and responsibility to the successor over a period of time. Eventually, over the course of several years, the new successor is fully in charge.

- **Advantages**—The successor accumulates experience gradually and can grow into the leadership position. This also allows the outgoing leader more time to consider their postwork options. It will also provide time to identify what support the successor will need in terms of management bench strength and governance, which will likely be different than it was for the predecessor. These specific needs are difficult to define early in the succession process.
- **Drawbacks**—A longer time frame means more possible tension and potential for of disagreement. For instance, some may question how a successor handles a new responsibility. Also, the current leader may feel as though they are being shoved aside if the successor appears overly eager to take command.

5. Transfer to a Nonfamily CEO (interim or longer term)

With this choice, the current leader transfers control to a nonfamily CEO. As the outgoing leader gradually transitions out, the nonfamily member serves as a mentor to the successor, who eventually takes charge over a period of upwards of several years.

- **Advantages**—This strategy can be quite helpful for successors who are not fully prepared to take charge. A nonfamily member can also introduce changes and innovations more easily than a younger, less-experienced family member. It may be that the nonfamily member is the best choice for the position, and will serve the shareholders' needs better than any family member can (at least for the present time.)
- **Disadvantages**—Family members sometimes struggle with this, particularly if it is the first time in the history of the business that a nonfamily CEO is developed or recruited.

We clearly favor the gradual/progressive strategy. Although by no means perfect, it offers the most reliable road to a smooth and successful transition. Not only does it allow sufficient time for the successor to fully develop into an accomplished leader, it also provides the outgoing leader with ample opportunity to map out a rewarding retirement.

Contingency Plans

In some instances, leadership development doesn't go according to plan. Perhaps a favored candidate or candidates don't work out, or it becomes evident their development is going to take longer than initially anticipated. Or, the current leader has to exit earlier than expected for unforeseen reasons.

In these and other similar situations, contingency plans can prove invaluable in not merely keeping the business on track but allowing adequate time to address the situation. As we outlined in the prior section, you may wish to consider bringing in a qualified outsider. How long that person may remain in leadership depends on the situation as well as their willingness to be flexible. For instance, an outsider may prove to be a stopgap as well as a mentor to a member of the next generation, serving only several years until the successor is ready to take the reins. In other settings, when it becomes clear that no one is even remotely close to being ready, a leader may prove to be much more than a stopgap, serving a number of years until completely new candidates can be selected and developed. In one situation we know of, a member of the board stepped in as an interim leader while the family conducted an extensive search. Because they had someone close to the company whom they trusted, they felt they could take the time to select carefully.

The Importance of Creativity and Transparency

Here is an example of a complex leadership change that illustrates the value of contingency planning as well as transparency. We recently worked with a company transitioning from the fourth to the fifth generation. The business itself was also changing its focus from home building to real estate development. The business, which employed 10 family members and had 50 shareholders, had never had a nonfamily CEO.

One central issue was uncertainty about whether most of the family who had grown up in home building would be capable of executing the new direction. To help address that, we developed a shareholder survey to determine how to gauge the importance of family leadership. Most felt it would be suitable to have a family chairman so long as the nonfamily CEO was a good cultural fit. From there, we established a skill profile, engaged an outside search firm, and interviewed family and nonfamily candidates using the same process.

Through each step, we made certain that all shareholders knew exactly what was going on and at what point we were in the overall process. We also provided updates at each board meeting. In the end, they opted for a family CEO, supported by a nonfamily COO and a family CFO. It was a challenging transition, but one that went more smoothly because the process was transparent and everyone was informed along the way.

The Value of Thoughtful Proactivity

Here are two examples of companies that underscore the importance of proactive leadership continuity planning in a variety of ways. One business had been planning for the eventual transition of a younger-generation member into the leadership role for several years. Members of the organization's management team were all aware of this planned transition, and all voiced support for the heir apparent. This endorsement was critical to the successor's successful transition. It also underscored that he had been very well prepared.

Several steps were taken to ensure that the successor had the knowledge and experience necessary to run the business, including

- attendance of industry functions for a number of years and a resulting level of recognition and respect;
- interaction with customers and vendors;
- experience running the purchasing and warehouse areas of the business; and
- exposure to branch operations.

During the planning for this leadership transition, we also recommended a number of additional steps to help ensure that the transition went smoothly and that the successor was as fully prepared as possible. One of these was self-assessment and identification of certain personal goals. In addition to the organizational goal of ensuring that he had the skills and experience required to successfully run the company, the successor identified a set of personal goals that he wished to achieve. They included

- improving work habits (e.g., avoid procrastination, time management, task prioritization);
- building confidence;
- establishing a mentor network to support him during and after the transition; and

- creating a conflict resolution process that could be used to address points of disagreement.

With respect to skills and experience, the successor had already had significant exposure to many areas of the business, both internally and externally (i.e., purchasing, warehouse, industry associations). While his knowledge of these areas continued to grow, the overall transition was also designed to provide exposure to other areas with which he was less familiar (e.g., sales, finance, human resources). Everything came together, as the transition into leadership proved smooth and successful.

At Abarta (mentioned in Chapter 2), management also moved very proactively to plan for leadership succession, although, in this case, things did not turn out precisely as they had anticipated. In fact, when the company began considering planning for long-term leadership continuity in 1990, then-CEO John Bitzer Jr. was unsure when he planned to retire. Nonetheless, he knew it was critical to get a jump on leadership continuity.

The first step was the development of a "succession committee" comprised of the board of directors and advisers. They were charged with developing the criteria for top management leadership. It was decided that the process would involve testing three specific candidates for varied strengths and weaknesses. It was also agreed that the sharing of plans for personal development would also be a keystone. The committee believed this would be an effective means of building trust. The succession committee also planned other activities, such as team-building trips, developing mentor relationships, and other programs.

Ultimately, after a period of several years, the process culminated in determining that all three candidates initially singled out as possible successors were not quite ready to take over the CEO position. As a result, Bitzer remained in his position for several more years as the leadership continuity program continued. Eventually, one of the three candidates did, in fact, assume the position of CEO, but, thanks to the proactivity of the overall process, only did so after taking several more years to grow into the job.[3]

Leadership continuity planning is exciting, and requires intense discussion among management, the board, and the family. However, like other aspects of family business continuity, the long-term benefits are well worth the energy and effort, and it is a process that, if given the proper attention, can be extremely rewarding for all participants.

In Brief

- Leadership continuity planning is important to ensure a viable business with strong leadership.
- Leadership continuity planning starts with assessing the future challenges and opportunities your business will face, and in turn identifying the skill sets required to navigate the future.
- Careful attention should be paid to mapping the skills of leadership candidates with the skills required of the business. This assessment is then used to develop a plan for candidates to fill gaps in their skills and experience so that they will be well-qualified to lead when the time comes.
- Start the leadership development process early to find time to identify suitable candidates and to develop necessary skills.
- Mentors can be very valuable in helping promote leadership continuity.
- Ensure that attention is given to communication of the process, plans, progress, and outcomes.

Leadership Transition Plan

Project Objectives

Primary

Prepare Joe to take over the responsibility for running Allen Distribution in three to five years by
- developing a detailed action plan and timeline to support transition;
- creating a development plan to build skills and experience.

Secondary

Identify other elements to support a successful transition (e.g., organization structure, communication plan, family governance).
Clarify Dad's role at the time of the transition.

Steps Taken To Date

The Allen family has been proactive in planning for the eventual ownership and leadership transition of Allen Distribution from the first- to the second generation.

Ownership transition

The first generation has two goals in ownership transition: to move majority control of Allen Distribution into the hands of the immediate family, and to pass stock to the second generation. To achieve these goals, the first generation has established an annual gifting program. In addition, Joe has been purchasing treasury stock. While this plan will achieve the first of the two goals (majority control), it is unlikely to achieve movement of all of the first-generation stock to the second generation or to fund Dad's retirement. A high-level plan has thus been developed that outlines the timing and mechanism for transferring the remainder of the stock, taking into account the retirement needs of the first generation. This plan calls for Joe to begin purchasing Dad's stock with his annual bonus, once he has purchased enough stock to obtain majority control. This plan needs to be fleshed out, with input from a trusted, qualified financial adviser in order to ensure that both generations are fully aware and comfortable with financial aspects (tax, personal, insurance, and so forth).

While it is the primary goal of this report to deal with leadership transition, I believe it is important to note this critical action item from an ownership transition standpoint. I recommend that the family meet as soon as possible to discuss the ownership transition plan.

Leadership transition

The family has been planning for Joe's eventual transition into the leadership role at Allen Distribution for several years. Members of the organization's management team are all aware of this transition. They all voice their support of Joe and are confident that he will run the business well. This endorsement is critical to Joe's success and suggests that Joe has been well prepared.

Several steps have been taken to ensure that Joe has the knowledge and experience necessary to run the business:
- He has attended industry functions for a number of years and is recognized and respected in the industry.
- He has interacted with customers and vendors.

- He has run the purchasing and warehouse areas of the business.
- He has been exposed to branch operations.

This report will outline additional steps that should be taken to ensure that Joe is prepared to take over the business in the designated timeframe.

Goals for Leadership Transition

In addition to the organization goal of ensuring that he has the skills and experience required to successfully run Allen Distribution, Joe has identified a set of personal goals that he would like to achieve. They include

- improving work habits (e.g., avoid procrastination, time management, task prioritization);
- building self-confidence;
- establishing a mentor network to support him during and after the transition;
- creating a conflict resolution process that can be used to address areas in which Joe and Dad disagree.

With respect to skills and experience, Joe has already had significant exposure to many areas of the business, both internal and external (i.e., purchasing, warehouse, industry associations). While his knowledge of these areas will continue to grow, the goal of this transition plan is to provide exposure to the remaining areas (for example, sales, finance, HR). *It is assumed that he will retain oversight responsibility for other areas (not day-to-day operating responsibility) while he builds his experience in new areas.*

Leadership Transition Plan Steps

1. Relinquish hands-on operating responsibilities to provide time to learn key aspects of the business

Action	Completion date	Responsibility	Update	New Completion date
Hire warehouse manager or at least more help in warehouse	7/31/04	Joe *primary* Dad *approve*	DONE	
Retain management responsibility for warehouse and purchasing			DONE	
Write Joe's job description as related to purchasing and warehouse	7/31/04	Joe *primary* Dad *approve*	DONE	

2. Learn key aspects of running the business

a. Understand finances and develop financial management and budgeting skills

Action	Completion date	Responsibility	Update	New Completion date
Meet with accountant to review 2003 audited financials	7/31/04	Joe *primary* Dad *support*		3/31/06
Meet with Dad or accountants monthly to review month-end financials, including A/R aging (at lunch meeting)	ongoing	Joe *primary* Dad *support*		
Meet with bankers to understand financing and accounts	9/30/04	Joe *primary* Dad *support*	DONE	
Take a class in managerial accounting	12/31/04	Joe		

Action	Completion date	Responsibility	Update	New Completion date
Build *practice* budget for 2005 • gather assumptions from management team • review industry benchmarks	3/31/05	Joe		
Transition check-signing responsibility Joe	6/30/05	Joe		6/30/06
Take responsibility for overseeing A/R	6/30/05	Joe		

b. Understand key HR aspects of business and develop management skills

Action	Completion date	Responsibility	Update	New Completion date
Review benefits information with Rob	12/31/04	Joe	DONE	
Update employee manual with management team	12/31/04	Joe *secondary* Anne *primary*		6/30/06
Read book on procrastination and develop action plan to improve work style	12/31/04	Joe		
Take course in conflict resolution	12/31/04	Joe	DONE	
Build conflict resolution plan with Dad	12/31/04	Joe *primary* Dad *secondary*		

Action	Completion date	Responsibility	Update	New Completion date
Create long-term organization chart	3/31/05	Joe *primary* Dad *secondary*	DONE	
Develop plan to transition to long-term organization chart	3/31/05	Joe		6/30/06

c. Understand technology

Action	Completion date	Responsibility	Update	New Completion date
Meet with Dad and Rob to review key aspects of system and how it supports business	12/31/04	Joe		3/31/06
Attend final meeting with company providing canned program (if procured)	When occurs	Joe		
Participate in training on new system		Joe		
Attend meetings on system configuration of canned system, if procured		Joe		

3. Transition management responsibility
a. Increase direct line management responsibilities

Action	Completion date	Responsibility	Update	New Completion date
Transition phone and counter sales to Joe	6/30/06	Joe *primary* Dad *support*		12/31/06

Action	Completion date	Responsibility	Update	New Completion date
Update Joe's job description and communicate to the organization	6/30/06	Joe *primary* Dad *approve*		12/31/06
Transition monthly management meetings to Joe (set agenda, preside)	6/30/06	Joe		12/31/06

b. Transition full management authority

Action	Completion date	Responsibility	Update	New Completion date
Transition branch reporting to Joe	6/30/07	Joe *primary* Dad *support*		
Update Joe's job description and communicate to organization	6/30/07	Joe *primary* Dad *approve*		
Change Joe's title	12/31/07	Dad		
Have Joe's team in place	12/31/07	Joe *primary* Dad *approve*		
Dad stops regular attendance at monthly management meetings	12/31/07	Dad		
Set management agreement between Joe and Dad (periodic meeting schedule, conflict resolution process)	12/31/07	Joe Dad		
Write job description for Dad	6/30/07	Dad *primary* Joe *support*		
Transition banker, accountant, other relationships	6/30/07	Dad *primary* Joe *support*		

4. Build additional skills and infrastructure to support transition

a. Build leadership skills

Action	Completion date	Responsibility	Update	New Completion date
Develop vision statement	12/31/04	Joe *primary* Dad *support*		3/31/06
Build performance management system	3/31/05	Joe *primary* Dad *support*		
Complete 2006 budget	12/31/05	Joe		
Identify leadership opportunities in community	12/31/05	Joe		
Clarify long-term financial goals for the business	6/30/06	Joe *primary* Dad *support*		12/31/06
Develop strategic plan	12/31/06	Joe *primary* Dad *support*		

b. Develop mentor network

Action	Completion date	Responsibility	Update	New Completion date
Identify areas for mentor support (leadership skills, financial management skills, other)	8/31/04	Joe	DONE	
Identify potential mentor candidates (extended family, industry, family business, community)	9/30/04	Joe	DONE	
Recruit mentors	10/31/04	Joe		
Establish regular meeting schedule with mentors	12/31/04	Joe		

c. Create family governance process

Action	Completion date	Responsibility	Update	New Completion date
Review estate and retirement planning at family meeting	8/31/04	Dad	DONE	
Hold monthly family meetings with 4 family members	Ongoing	All		
Develop agenda for family meetings (review financials, review succession plan, other)	Ongoing	Joe/Anne		
Hold quarterly family meetings, including spouses	Ongoing	All		
Attend Family Business Academy	6/30/05	Joe		
Create plan to work with other Allen Appliance companies • get input from other Allen family members • hold meeting with families	6/30/06	Joe *primary* Dad *support*	IN PROCESS	

Family Member Time Line (2008–2016)

	Year	2008	2009	2010	2011	2012	2013	2014	2015	2016
Anthony Smith (G2)	Position	President							Chairman	
	Age	55							62	
Joe Daniels (G2)		Division VP 52							President 59	
Rich Carmichael (G2)		Division VP 49								
Outside President										
Jim Smith	Age		26		28				32	
	Possible Position		Engineer		Project mgr				Marketing	
Ann Daniels	Age		25		27				31	
	Possible Position		Engineer		Project mgr				Finance	

Year	2008	2009	2010	2011	2012	2013	2014	2015	2016
Jay Smith									
Age					26	27			
Possible Position					Engineer	Project mgt			
John Carmichael									
Age					26	27			
Possible Position					Engineer	Project mgr			
Chris Carmichael									
Age									26
Possible Position									Engineer
Jason Daniels									
Age									
Possible Position									

107

Family Member Time Line (2017–2025)

Year	2017	2018	2019	2020	2021	2022	2023	2024	2025
Anthony Smith (G2) — Position			Retired						
Age			66						
Joe Daniels (G2)			Chairman 63			Retired 66			
Rich Carmichael (G2)			President 60			Chairman 63			retired 66
Outside President						President			
Jim Smith — Age						39	40	41	42
Possible Position									President?
Ann Daniels — Age						38	39	40	41
Possible Position									President?

108

	Year	2017	2018	2019	2020	2021	2022	2023	2024	2025
Jay Smith										
Age			32							
Possible Position			HR							
John Carmichael										
Age			32							
Possible Position			Construction mgt							
Chris Carmichael										
Age			28					33		
Possible Position			Project mgr					TBD		
Jason Daniels										
Age		26		28					33	
Possible Position		Engineer		Project mgt					TBD	

109

5

The Role of Business Governance in Continuity Planning

An effective form of governance is of great value in helping family members make sound decisions. The term "governance" refers to the process and structure for oversight and decision-making. In family businesses, there are two distinct realms in which governance is critical—the family and the business. In this chapter we will discuss the essential role that well-structured business governance (sometimes referred to as corporate governance) plays in the success of any family business.

Without effective business governance, decision-making becomes more challenging, accountability can suffer, and an entire organization can wrestle with a lack of focus and common purpose. Beyond its important role in the day-to-day decision-making, a well-designed business governance structure and process is crucial to ensuring that succession occurs in a smooth, thoughtfully orchestrated manner.

For many family entities, a board of directors is the core component of business governance. However, for those businesses that don't have a board of directors—or one that only exists on paper—there is still a need for a decision-making structure to provide day-to-day oversight and accountability and, most important, to oversee continuity planning to ensure an effective business transition across generations. For some families, the continuity planning process may be overseen by family members in management. Others may have periodic meetings with owners, family, and/or outside advisers to discuss issues related to the longer term of the business.

Regardless of the level of formality of your decision-making structure, it is important to ensure there are a place, a process, ownership, and accountability for managing the continuity planning process. Too often, families overlook continuity planning because they have not defined a means to manage it effectively.

Board of Directors' Role—An Overview

The term "governance" is defined by the dictionary as control or authority. Corporate or business governance is used more broadly to define the structure and processes of overseeing a business to ensure accountability of management and effective decision-making. For many businesses, a board of directors is the central means of business governance.

The function of a board in family businesses varies widely. The responsibilities of an active and engaged board of directors can include

- review of company performance and identification of issues that warrant attention;
- holding management accountable for achieving strategic, operational, and financial objectives;
- evaluation of strategic alternatives;
- review, evaluation, and approval of strategic planning;
- review of operating and capital budgets;
- oversight and direction to help owners develop clear vision and objectives; and
- evaluation of the performance of senior management.

Family businesses that survive and prosper have solid decision-making processes, sufficient oversight to ensure management accountability, processes to address crises in the business as well as management, and a smooth leadership and ownership succession process. An active and engaged board helps ensure all those things happen.

Specific to the issue of continuity, a board can be of invaluable help and guidance in a variety of ways.

The Board's Role in Strategic Planning

The strategic plan outlines goals for the business and the plans to achieve those goals. The planning process may include a review of key competitors and trends in the marketplace that will affect the business over time. A sound strategic plan is designed to evaluate the opportunities and threats presented to the business and devise a set of actions to address them so that the business can meet its goals. While strategic planning is an important element of an effective business at any given moment, it is crucial in times of generational transition. Often, members of an elder generation are hesitant to leave the business in the hands of the next generation. With a well-crafted strategic plan, the retiring generation can have confidence that management is aligned to achieve its goals. The board plays an important role in ensuring management has developed a sound strategic plan and in tracking progress against that plan. In fact, elder-generation members may sit on the board that reviews the plan, creating more confidence that the business is well managed. The strategic planning process can also be a way for family businesses with multiple family members who are active in the business to ensure their alignment on the long-term direction of the business. In addition, it provides an opportunity for nonfamily management to play an integral role in developing a roadmap for the future of the business.

With some of our clients, a decision is made to hold off on defining the profile for the next-generation business leader until a strategic plan is developed. In one case, members retiring from the business in the near future were wise to recognize that their core business was changing. Until they defined their desires with respect to what markets they would pursue in the future, they didn't know what leadership skills and experience would be most valuable.

If you have not developed a strategic plan for your business, it would useful for your organization to do so. The strategic plan serves as a vehicle to articulate to multiple constituents (board, management, bankers, and family members) where the business is headed, at least for the next several years:

- It educates those same groups about the industry, and how the family business is positioned within that industry.

- It fosters support and empathy from family members who are not in the business and who, as a result, realize the complexity of remaining competitive in the industry.
- It allows everyone to get on the same page in terms of the direction in which efforts must be focused.

The Board's Role in Leadership Development

The ultimate responsibility of the board is to ensure the business is well run. To do so, they need to rely on a sound management team. The board plays a crucial role in leadership succession planning by evaluating current management, considering the leadership needs of the business in the future (based on its goals as defined in the strategic plan), and overseeing the development of new leaders. The board also has ultimate responsibility for selecting the next leader of the business, typically specified in the corporate by-laws. Long before a transition is to occur, the board should be working with management to ensure that everything is being done to prepare a suitable successor. Moreover, if independent members are present on the board, they can play an invaluable role in providing objective feedback on the capabilities and development of both family and nonfamily successors.

Capable directors will understand the value of sound leadership succession planning long before a leader needs to be selected. Independent director Steve Tourek at Marvin Windows and Doors has been active in the development of a leadership evaluation and development process for the next generation of Marvin leaders. Put into place in 2003 and spearheaded by nonfamily board members, the program involves a series of self-assessment exercises through which family members evaluate their strengths, goals, motivations, and other aspects of their lives. When the process began, Tourek notes that family members of varied ages took part: "Some of them were in their forties and already working in the company, while others were still in their teens."

The goal of the program—which culminates with participants writing a narrative describing themselves—is to allow family members to gain a better understanding of their personal and professional attributes and, should they wish to work within the company, where those characteristics might best fit. Not only does the program target family members who have leadership potential, which can then be developed and nurtured, but it also allows family members to find roles that will prove most enjoyable and rewarding. "If they know from the beginning where they envision their career going and where they could be matched with the needs of the business, it increases the odds of a successful outcome," says Tourek. "It's beneficial for the business as well as the health and happiness of family members."

With the board's oversight, the program has also been modified as needed for family members who are not comfortable with self-assessment: "We just go straight into the interview and just let them talk. The interviewer then writes the narrative for them."

The Board's Role in Ownership Succession

The transition of shares in the family business is typically governed by the owners themselves, who decide to whom they will give or sell shares. However, the board plays an important role in urging owners to think through the development of a smooth and orderly process for this transition. Again, the board's role is to ensure the health of the business. If the transition of shares is not carefully planned, it can affect business viability. What if one branch of the family has failed to set aside sufficient funds for estate taxes? If someone from that part of the family passes away, they may have to sell shares to pay the tax. Even worse, if no one else has the funds or access to funds to buy the shares, the whole business can be placed in jeopardy.

An involved board of directors can help make certain these critical aspects of continuity are not overlooked. A proactive board can remind family members of the importance of setting aside enough money to retire comfortably. If they're assuming that they're going to continue to receive a salary after they retire, the board needs to ensure that the business has the financial wherewithal to support the additional cost.

The Value of Board Members as Mentors

Many board members have years of valuable experience they are eager to share. They can serve a family business' continuity planning by acting as mentors to younger family members. Not only can they pass along the insights and wisdom they have acquired over time, but they can also work closely with members of the younger generations to help them understand the skills and experience they will need to acquire in order to assume ownership and leadership roles in the future. This relationship can also prove more comfortable with younger family members who may be reticent to bring up issues or ask certain questions of their parents or some other older family member.

Interestingly, mentoring relationships can also occur with older family members. We've seen situations in which board members serve as a mentor and adviser to a retiring CEO, helping them to realize why it's time for them to move on and allow younger family members the opportunity to step up. In addition, board incumbent directors also serve that role for incoming CEOs. One nonfamily CEO, new to the position, commented: "Having informed and experienced (in our business) board members really helped accelerate my learning curve as the new leader of the business—I was really grateful for that support and guidance."

The Board's Role in Enforcing Ownership Vision and Goals

Aligning a family's vision and values with the business means not merely making certain that everyone involved is aware of those values and embraces them but also that major company programs, decisions, and other activities are consistent with those values. A board can encourage family members to sit down and take the time needed to formally draw up a statement of vision and values. Moreover, it's important that those values are reflected in a company's continuity plan and other decisions regarding continuity. For example, if continuity planning involves selecting a future CEO, and a core business value is that the family always wants a family member in that position, the board can serve as something of a fail-safe to help guide the family in selecting a successor consistent with that value. In that sense, the board can serve as something of a decision "rudder," making certain that significant decisions impacting continuity are made in accordance with family vision and priorities.

Not only can a board help ensure that a suitable and effective continuity plan is in place, but it can provide assurance that all important decisions are made in accordance with the family's continuity objectives and values. For instance, if the board knows that the goal of the family is to keep the business in the family, they can then recommend steps the business would do well to take to make sure that occurs—and, by the same token, point out potential decisions that would run counter to that value. That can include anything from setting out clear guidelines as to what requirements will be in place to work in the business to making certain that younger family members receive the training and support they will need to develop into solid leaders and owners.

The Optimal Board for Continuity Issues

Boards vary in the specifics of their composition. We recommend a board comprised of independent directors as well as family members as the most effective makeup to take on the challenges of continuity planning and execution.

Independent directors are valuable in continuity planning because they're unbiased in terms of whom they may deem suitable for assuming key leadership roles in the business. In fact, we have surveyed family businesses with regard to their level of satisfaction with their board of directors. Overall, businesses that had boards that included independent directors felt that their boards were more helpful in successfully running their business than those whose boards did not include independent directors. It seems evident that independent directors help make everyone more accountable, more prepared, and work with a greater level of professionalism and objectivity.

That's been the case at McKee Foods Corp, manufacturer of the well-known Little Debbie's snacks. In particular, company president, Mike McKee, says the introduction of independent members to their board in 2008 has greatly increased overall accountability: "Before we had a board of directors with outsiders, we really didn't feel we had to answer to anyone."

Independent directors can be particularly helpful in support of continuity planning by helping family members make decisions that are not biased by personal interests, conflict, or history. Additionally, although leadership and ownership transitions are not everyday occurrences, independent directors may have experienced them in the past. That can provide valuable guidance and insight, particularly with an objective evaluation of management talent.

Just as important, independent directors (and a board of directors in general) are charged with looking at the business with an ongoing regard to a long-term perspective. That means their work as a board is consistently characterized by a focus on continuity.

That makes the selection of independent directors an important responsibility. If you're thinking about adding independent directors to your board, think about the ideal profile of an independent director to help you through continuity planning For instance, if your company is in real estate, the natural conclusion would be to look for independent directors experienced in real estate issues. The potential problem here is that, while a person may be knowledgeable about real estate, they may not be familiar enough with the dynamics of your business to help with continuity issues. They may not be an effective mentor. As an alternative, it might be more suitable to look for a candidate who may not be as well versed in real estate, but who has been through a generational transition or has solid mentoring skills. We suggest that, while industry experts on your board can add real value because they speak your language, at the same time, you are already industry experts as insiders. Board composition should represent a diverse group of directors who bring multiple skills from a broad experience base.

Designing a Board to Support Leadership Transition

Nixon Medical is unique in a number of ways. It has come a long way since 1967, when Murray Berstein and his brother bought a dry cleaner—a good deal removed from the textile rental service that now serves some 5,000 customers each week in the Northeast and the mid-Atlantic.

But what also separates Nixon from many other family-owned businesses is its early establishment of a board of directors and the critical role it played in the leadership transition from Murray to his sons, Jason, Dan, and Ben, that began in 2007.

"It was unique for a business with revenues under $10 million to decide to establish a board of directors for guidance," says Dan Berstein, who with Jason and Ben owns the company in equal shares. "But our father certainly leaned on the board. They were very involved in the process of selecting Jason as the qualified leader."

But the board's value in the transition from Murray to Jason went beyond setting up an empirical selection and decision-making processes. For both Ben and Dan, the board's involvement provided essential confidence in the continuity process as well as the choice of Jason as successor.

"In the absence of having the board, it would be more challenging for me to empower a single qualified leader without some oversight," says Ben. "It lets me stay in my managerial role. I have trust there is appropriate oversight there. At the end of the day, Jason has accountability to the board whose members are elected by the three of us. It helped us to get through the transition emotionally."

"They play a more important role now than they did in establishing that process," adds Dan. "The role they play now allows the model we have to really function well. We have our voice—our voice is in the election of our directors. We can function in our roles better."

Nor is Nixon's continuity planning limited to board activities. The family meets three times a year to discuss various aspects of the business, including continuity issues.

"It's amazing to us how far in advance that you need to plan so emotions aren't involved," says Dan. "Every year we qualify and plan for Nixon to remain 100 percent family owned. We communicate that to our executive team and to the board.

"The second day of the retreat includes our spouses, so they're also aligned. We've started to prepare for conversations about children entering the business. We kind of agreed—not formally—about the requirement of first having a job outside the business before you join our business. You're not going to get a job at Nixon in a senior role just because you're a family member. You're going to get that if you're qualified for the job."

Jason's successful ascension to the leadership role at Nixon is a testament to the company's commitment to a thoughtful and effective continuity process. As Dan notes, while Jason and Murray have both occupied the same chair, their leadership styles are very different.

"Jason is a very different leader than our father was. Our father was involved in the details of growing a dry cleaner with four employees. He was very detailed oriented," says Dan. "Jason is much more of a business strategist who relies on having the right people in the right position. I don't know that Jason's style would have worked in accomplishing what our father accomplished, and I'm not sure our father was prepared to take the business to the next level."

The Importance of Family Directors in Continuity Planning

Independent directors are undoubtedly valuable. But it's just as beneficial also to have family members on your board as there are many things they can contribute to the overall quality of the planning process. For one thing, it can be an intimidating idea for nonfamily employees to experience a generational transition. Perhaps they enjoyed working for the senior generation, but now that the elder generation is retiring and one of their children is taking over, nonfamily management may worry that the wheels are going to come off. Siblings and cousins have the same concern about a "peer" leader. They have no idea whether everybody is going to get along when senior-generation members are not there to break ties or provide the last word on an important decision. They fear the siblings who aren't chosen as CEO may quit or attempt to undermine the success of the chosen leader if they stay.

Therein lies a significant advantage to family board members. Knowing that there are family members who are on the board who are caring and aware of the varied issues involved in the transition can provide great peace of mind. They build confidence among members of nonfamily management that the family is trying to build harmony and is working to manage the whole process as effectively as possible.

Family board members can also be particularly aware of family dynamics. They can be sensitive as to how to communicate decisions that spare individuals' feelings. They can also provide a conduit to communicate with other family members who aren't on the board.

Recently, we spoke with a client who greatly valued the independent directors on the board. However, he said that it was critical to have them sitting alongside family directors who knew the family's history and "baggage" from the past and could guide independent directors in understanding politics and animosities that may affect owners and family employees' behavior.

It's often difficult to find family directors who possess all the skills and experience required to serve as a strong director. At the same time, independent directors—at least as newcomers—cannot understand the complex history associated with the family that has contributed to the current dynamics. That makes the marriage of the skills, experience, and perspective of both types of directors invaluable.

Like an independent director, it is critical to choose the family member best suited to contribute to a board's involvement in continuity planning and execution. First, the family member must understand that their role is to represent the family as a whole, rather than particular branches or segments of the family or, worse yet, a personal agenda. Moreover, they should be well respected by the entire family for their solid communication skills and good judgment. Last, they should possess a sense for when to speak up and when to recuse themselves from certain decisions.

No matter the specific composition of a board, we generally recommend that boards be fiduciary in nature rather than merely advisory. That can help bolster accountability as well as the board's authority in providing effective oversight of the business, in continuity matters as well as a variety of other issues.

The Importance of Board Continuity

An engaged board of directors can prove critical in helping to ensure smooth and effective continuity throughout all parts of a family business. Just as important is the challenge of ensuring smooth continuity on the board itself.

As we have noted, many boards are comprised of independent directors as well as family members. However, no matter the specific makeup of the board, it is important to bear in mind that the board, however effective and involved, will not remain intact indefinitely. Some directors may retire, others may opt out for other commitments, some may leave due to term limits, and still others may simply prove to be ineffective board members.

That means change is always an issue to be addressed. That raises the question: "Who is thinking about preparing and making sure that we have qualified directors in the next generation and qualified outsiders?" That's a question that many of our clients do not consider early on. Their inattention is understandable. They are so focused on running the business that they overlook that, in several years' time, they're going to have several openings on their board of directors. As the retirement of family members or independent directors approaches, they come to understand the importance of assembling a capable group of people ready and able to assume positions on the board.

We have seen several cases of families ignoring the fact that directors are aging and perhaps becoming less effective or involved in the boardroom. Often, the issue comes to a head when the elder generation isn't ready to resign from the board to make way for members of the next generation. Thoughtful consideration of how to prepare the next generation to cycle onto the board is warranted, particularly because the next generation almost always has more members than the current board requires.

This is a particular challenge when the board is comprised of all owners. With a generational transition, the board would be too large. That means the family needs to select among next-generation members to serve. At Highlights for Kids, the owners developed a process in which next-generation members serve as observers on the board for two years. They start with the oldest and move through the rotation until the youngest has served. This experience is invaluable in preparing next-generation directors as well as educating owners about the business.

Training and preparation can occur in a number of ways. For instance, family meetings can be ideal settings to help educate younger family members about the business. In participating, they begin to acquire the knowledge and tools possibly to be board members in the future. Another setting is a board meeting itself. These can provide opportunities for younger family members to attend and observe a meeting without actually taking part in the meeting.

Many families understand the value of orientation or a summer internship program in the business. The same thinking should hold true for the board of directors, especially with family members who may never wish to work in the business, but may, in fact, be highly suitable board members. The family can develop a training or board development program that meets the needs of both the business and the family.

The board should also consider continuity of the chair. The chair is an exceedingly important position, not only in function but also as a representative and the voice of family values. Unfortunately, relatively few families give thought to the issue of continuity in this critical role. Yet just as you should pay due attention to the continuity of your overall board, you must also consider succession in the critical capacity of board chair. It is particularly important to envision what you expect the chair to do—maintain family harmony, defuse potentially explosive situations, serve as a communication link between board and family, plan for and facilitate effective meetings. Board continuity also requires a clear set of guidelines and parameters as to who can serve on the board and what sorts of qualifications, background, and experience are required for board service. You will need to consider whether you want various elements of the family represented equally or by ownership share, who will nominate family directors, who will select them, and how you will capture these expectations in writing so that all family members have a mutual understanding of the process and requirements.

Continuity Challenges? Build a Board!

Many families who are confronting continuity issues may be doing so without the support and valued guidance of a board. Fortunately, that can change.

The leadership succession process often proves to be a catalyst for putting a board of directors in place. Several clients have engaged us to help them establish a board of directors because the business was poised to move from one generation to the next. Having addressed that process on their own in the past, they had determined a board would be helpful. For other clients, the trigger derives from considering a non-family CEO for the first time. In that situation, they want to make sure they have independent directors who are charged with making certain the new leader follows the family's values, vision, and overall objectives. A board can provide oversight to ensure the leader is accomplishing his job, both in terms of meeting business expectations as well as family expectations. Another motivation for the development of a board is the increased complexity of the business—it might be growing rapidly, be threatened by emerging competitors, or not be meeting planned objectives. In these cases, a board can help ensure the continuity of the business by providing valuable strategic insight.

The Board's Role in Supporting Continuity

Many clients also see a board as effective in stewarding continuity issues beyond the time of a leadership or ownership transition. Biscuitville, a chain of 50 restaurants in North Carolina and Virginia, is one such business. As founder Maurice Jennings gradually became less involved in the business, his son and successor, Burney, and his siblings decided to establish a board well in advance of their father's departure to ensure that everyone continued to behave as they had when "Dad was in the room." In that instance, the board aided not only in the continuity process itself but also in perpetuating an optimal boardroom culture and determining the division of responsibilities of among owners, family, and business.

"The whole purpose for setting up the board was ensuring continuity from the first to the second generations," explains Burney Jennings. "We were concerned about succession issues because, in our case, the business was not passed to just one person."

Biscuitville also took a thoughtful approach to building a board. Jennings encouraged shareholders to take the lead in interviewing and selecting board members: "It was my belief that, if I approached the shareholders and told them I was setting up a board of directors, at the end of the day they wouldn't have any ownership of it. The shareholders handled the interviews and made the decisions. I participated, but as one of the shareholders, not as the CEO."

Jennings also expects the board to address succession issues in the near future: "The board will be focusing on family members coming into the business. I have four kids and my sister has two. The board will be active in making certain they're qualified, determining how much they'll be paid, and overseeing their path of entry into the business."

Perhaps the optimal situation in establishing a board for the first time is one in which a family business recognizes well in advance that there will be continuity issues and challenges— as much as several years prior to the expected changeover.

Here's how that might play out. A family business expects a transition in five to ten years. Many family members are aware and perhaps concerned that the process of developing a continuity plan and the execution of that plan might have some bumps along the road. What might they be doing now? One solution is to put a board in place well in advance of the time when the transition is slated to occur. Given that it's very early in the process, things are likely be a good deal less contentious, since everyone involved can begin thinking about important issues and decisions before things become a good deal more emotional. An involved board of directors can encourage that sort of proactive thinking.

That can prove particularly true with first-generation entrepreneurs, who may feel that a board is unnecessary, needlessly formal, or will simply slow down decision-making. Such a wary entrepreneur can be convinced of the value of a board with the argument that her children will likely put a board into place after she has stepped down. If such a move is inevitable, wouldn't she rather participate in the transition to an active board? The board will benefit from getting to know her and understanding her vision and aspirations for the business once she's no longer in the driver's seat.

In terms of formality, family members often envision boards as forums for discussing issues and voting on many decisions. As a matter of fact, boards in privately held companies rarely vote and can be quite informal. Most decisions are arrived at by consensus—the group reviews material in advance of a meeting on a topic that might require a decision, it is discussed at the board, and decisions can be reached without a formal vote.

A board can tackle issues and problems well before they become more serious issues. That sort of "preventive maintenance" might not happen in family businesses without a board asking questions in a proactive manner. The analogy of a flu shot is compelling. If you receive a flu shot well in advance of flu season, you're doing everything you can to avoid the misery of getting sick. By contrast, receiving a flu shot when you're already achy and running a fever isn't going to do you much good. The same dynamic holds true with a board. The sooner it is in place, the more good it can accomplish. In addition, a decision-making group can engage in more rational analysis when the business is healthy and the family dynamics are positive.

The topic of putting a board into place before continuity issues are at your doorstep centers on the core consideration of how you want succession decisions to be made, who you want to be involved in the process, and how you plan to oversee the transition process. In that sense, it also broadens your view of what a board can do. You start to think about the board through a lens that's not limited to strategic issues and financial statements, but as an entity that can help ensure the continuity of the business through effective management.

Here's an exercise to consider if you have not yet put a board in place. At your next family meeting or gathering, urge family members to take a few minutes to envision the business ten years in the future (or whatever time frame will likely coincide with the retirement of a key leader.) Challenge the family: What would they like to have in place with respect to the business and the family so that any significant challenges are addressed effectively? Moreover, what might they expect those challenges to be? Will one member of the family be envious of another who has been promoted quickly up the chain of command? Will one branch of the family own more shares, but still have no one in a key management position?

For many families, the logical answer to help address these and other important issues is an active and engaged board of directors. At the very least, if the family isn't ready for a formal board, they will be forced to think about how they are going to make these crucial decisions.

This exercise can also highlight an trait that hinders many family businesses—the tendency to avoid conflict. Many family members—particularly those who have been around for a while and have seen their share of family squabbles— know that conflict can be intensely painful and unsettling. As a result, they avoid it.

Although most people do not enjoy conflict, it can be a good deal less unpleasant if it is acknowledged and addressed well before it becomes destructive. If a family begins to talk about conflict proactively, they can come up with effective solutions to manage it, or at the very least, minimize the damage. Since the bumps in the road around continuity can sometimes create conflict or tension, a board can prove a powerful force in encouraging family members to consider potential issues of conflict proactively so they don't cause long-lasting family disputes or breakdowns. With regard to many family business challenges—continuity among them—a strong board will help the family manage conflict effectively.

Using Your Ownership Group to Support Continuity Planning

Many family businesses don't have a board of directors, or, if they do, it's basically inactive. Although we are strong proponents of a board of directors and firmly believe in the varied advantages it can offer family businesses, the fact remains that many businesses don't really see the need for a board of directors. They may be relatively small and feel that a board would be unnecessary for a rather modest organization. By contrast, more established businesses may have prospered through one person's entrepreneurial vision and energy—someone who might think that a board would merely get in the way.

If you don't have an operating board in place, a family business' ownership group can play a critical role to help ensure appropriate continuity planning. The ownership group can manage its involvement in continuity planning through periodic shareholder meetings or ownership gatherings. For instance, a business may be owned by a second generation with three siblings running the business. While they may not need or feel the need for a formal board of directors, it's a solid strategy for that small group of owners to get together once a year (or more often) and look at where the business is headed. Do they have the right people in place to run it? Are they thinking through all the things they need to do to pass down stock from generation to generation? What challenges will they face over the next several years? Are they prepared for them?

We make no secret of our belief in the value of a board with regard to all sorts of governance related issues, including those addressing continuity. However, even if you determine that a board isn't the way for you to go, you should recognize that the mechanics of corporate governance you already have in place afford you opportunities for thoughtful, proactive continuity planning.

In Brief

- The business governance structure plays an essential role in a family business' continuity planning, by ensuring plans are in place and overseeing their execution.

- For many businesses, the board of directors is the mechanism for business oversight. As a result, it's very involved in continuity planning.
- It is also important to address continuity planning for the board itself—ideally, with a board that includes both family and independent members.
- Businesses without boards can address continuity planning strategy through regular leadership meetings and other forms of open discussion and decision-making.
- The more proactive the continuity planning, the greater the likelihood of successful transitions.

6

The Role of Family Governance in Continuity Planning

Just as business governance serves to strengthen and enhance the value of the business through generational transitions, effective family governance serves much the same purpose for the family: it strengthens bonds, creates a forum for developing family protocols, and helps unite family members in their effort to realize a common future vision.

Family governance lies on a continuum, along which there are gradations of formality. For some families, particularly in the first and second generations, it might take the form of family meetings held on a regular basis, or even ad-hoc meetings, called when a issue needs to be addressed. For other families (often larger groups) family governance might be achieved through a representative body of that group, often called a family council (some families have other labels such as a family steering group, a family stewardship committee, or a family board). Whatever the name, this group serves large families by creating a small group of representatives that can act on behalf of the entire family.

Many families who operate family businesses—particularly relatively small families or those in earlier generations of ownership—often question what the value of family governance. Our inevitable answer—family governance at any level of formality provides substantial benefits. Throughout this chapter we will refer to the family council as the primary governing body for the family. However, your family may use another term, or simply have no term at all for the decision-making group within the family. Family governance need not be that formal. That said, developing some kind of infrastructure (family meetings, a committee, for example) that enables fair decision-making for the family supports family relationships and continuity.

Family councils can be used to address a number of issues and challenges specific to a family business. Many families maintain a family council even if they have sold their business, as a group that supports family decision-making around shared assets. Councils focus on a variety of initiatives, such as establishing an employment policy for working within the business, creating a procedure for informing family members about important business or family-related matters, generating vision and values statements with the family, and creating a code of conduct and other policies or protocols. These plans help guide family involvement and interaction, which contribute to maintaining a bond among family members.

However, if we were to boil down the value of a family council into one succinct summation, it would be that family councils help keep the family together. In that sense, a family council is all about continuity—consistently working to ensure continuity both within the business as well as the family.

The Purpose of a Family Council

While it is often easy to grasp the purpose of a business board, there is more ambiguity for most business-owning families about the purpose of a family council. In essence, family councils are formed to oversee the management of the family. In a way, it's akin to a board of directors. The difference is, the board is charged with overseeing and helping guide the business, while a family council does the same thing with the family.

Some of the varied responsibilities of family council include

- building and maintaining an understanding of family vision and values and creating family unity;
- celebrating family and embracing life, personal joy, shared fun, and celebrations as foundations of individual and family identity;
- speaking for the family on matters affecting family values, aspirations, and expectations, and communicating decisions of the family council to family members and the boards of family businesses and foundations;

- serving as the entity where all family members can share personal objectives, concerns, and ideas with reference to matters affecting family values, family unity, and business success;
- fostering opportunities for all family members who wish to participate and contribute in some way to overall family welfare;
- adopting policies governing council and family conduct as well as establishing the family's overall direction;
- educating family members on the business and preparing them to be involved owners and to make important decisions about their ownership; and
- Serving as a forum for addressing conflict or disagreement in the family, or for providing support to family members in need

These points offer an overview of some of the major functions and responsibilities of a family council. Substitute the terms "board of directors" and "business" for "family council" and "family," and it might help provide some clarity with respect to how the family council occupies a concomitant, complementary role to the responsibilities of the business board.

Another issue raised by families who don't have a family council is one of applicability. For instance, some may say their family is too small to require that sort of oversight or that family issues to date have been easier to address through more informal channels. Others may address family issues through the business governance structure, either the board or the management team. This is often the case in early stage family businesses.

Those are certainly valid points. Many business-owning families function very well for years without a family council. Yet a case can be made for forming a family council, even if the need for one isn't so apparent or immediate. One reason is the expected exponential growth of the family. Few families remain static in size. People get married, have children, remarry, and so on. The size of the family can grow very quickly, particularly from the second- to the third generations.

That growth brings complexities, particularly with regard to planning generational transitions. Some examples include ownership structure of the business, leadership, diversification, and estate planning. Growth also means greater diversity—diverse family values across branches, diverse economic aspirations, diverse views of leadership transitions in the business—a natural outcome as the family population grows. Managing those diverse opinions and emotions becomes a challenge, one that can be effectively addressed by a governing body geared specifically to that task.

Another way to look proactively at this issue is to examine the changing roles of subsequent generations. As a family grows, varying numbers of people from individual generations may be directly involved in the business. For instance, everyone from the first generation may have worked in the business. By the time the third generation becomes adults, fewer family members may be active in the business—if, indeed, any work in the business. An active council helps inform and educate family members about the business so they can perpetuate their stewardship of family assets and the family legacy. And, it provides an opportunity for family members who are not employees to fulfill meaningful roles in support of the business and the family.

The council also serves as a relief valve to the family business CEO. We find that family businesses run by members of the family often expect the business leader to take on responsibility for leading the family, an unrealistic expectation for a single family member.

As the business grows and prospers, it requires strong, focused leadership. With that growth comes added stress, much of it falling directly on the shoulders of the CEO and other senior management. With all that the CEO has to focus on, it can be an enormous relief to know that family issues are in the capable hands of another person or entity—in this case, the family council. Creating a family council with separate leadership also sends an important signal about separation of business and family issues, a distinction that is often blurred for families in business together.

From planning family gatherings to mapping out policies to address family squabbles before they explode, a family council can offer much-needed support to leadership that is focused on running the business. What is more, as a family grows both in size and diversity, it is a welcome form of support. The family council can also be useful to a nonfamily CEO as a channel through which the CEO can communicate with the family and vice versa.

Last, as the family grows, there may also be increased disparity in what family members know and understand about the business, the family history, their ownership, their wealth, and many other matters that are of shared interest. In a family business that has grown to include several branches of cousins, there are typically significant distinctions across branches within the family. For instance, some branches may talk about business every night around the dinner table, while other branches rarely discuss business. Neither is right or wrong, but the result is differing levels of understanding of and emotional attachment to the business. A family council can create opportunities for family members to learn and develop a shared level of understanding of what opportunities and challenges they face as stewards of the family enterprise.

What Can You Expect from Your Family Council?

Return on investment is often a relatively simple calculation for financial investments. The calculation is less definitive, and the return less tangible, for a family council. However, among our clients with strong family councils, we are told that continuity through generations would have been significantly threatened without the council to guide and support the family. Specifically, the "return" is in the form of a foundation that will not only withstand the inevitable quakes that all business-owning families endure but will also develop the social and emotional capital without which decisions for continuity planning cannot be made. A family council builds that capital with strengthened communication, increased connectedness between family members, and clarity of expectations of family members in various settings.

The council is often the cornerstone of an effective communication network in the family. Strong communication is a primary focus of the council for a number of reasons. First, communication can always be improved, and poor communication rarely results in decisions that are widely accepted. In addition, most business-owning families have at least one memory (and typically more) of a decision where poor communication between family members resulted in a bad outcome. For example, in the early stages of a family business, the founders might agree that all relatives should be paid the same, regardless of their role in the business or their abilities. However well intentioned, that decision can inevitably lead to disputes among family members who feel—rightly so—that they shouldn't receive the same level of compensation as another family member who has completely different responsibilities. An active family council is not only aware of this existing issue but can communicate the need for updated policies and salary structures so that the problem doesn't continue indefinitely into the future.

The same can hold true with employment policies that have welcomed all family members into the business regardless of experience or training. Again, a family council can communicate the importance of relevant policies and guidelines, establish a process for developing such guidelines, and help ensure compliance. In all of these examples, the council's work supports continuity, working to reach decisions and to communicate those decisions that may have hindered continuity in the past, and taking steps to ensure they are not repeated.

We often hear next-generation members say that they place great importance on communication, if for no other reason than to avoid repeating past mistakes. In addition, family members like to be sufficiently informed to avoid being surprised by hearing about a key decision or change in the business from someone other than their own family, or the nonfamily leader in the business. Communication also creates a level playing field across family branches As we mentioned earlier, there are interbranch distinctions in flow and frequency of communication; some branches communicate often, while others rarely communicate with each other.

One way to help ensure that communication remains important is to specifically earmark time at family meetings to convey important information to other family members and bring everyone up to speed, including on social and policy development issues. This can be done with the entire family (often referred to as the family assembly), or in small groups within the family assembly. Some families develop a family website, the construction and content of which can be overseen by the family council. This can be a convenient way to maintain a consistent and comprehensive flow of information to all branches of the family.

The family council can also develop important policies relating to communication. For instance, the council might determine what sort of communications tools to use, how often to convey information, and the specific details of what will actually be shared with other family members. As we will discuss in the section on council structure, many families earmark a specific committee to handle the responsibility of communication.

Closely related to the value of communication is the family council's role in strengthening the overall social fabric of the family. As a family grows and evolves, it often becomes more difficult to bring the family together. Strong communication fosters trust, and if family members lack a sense of connection and trust, continuity becomes increasingly difficult to plan and execute.

A family council can serve to bolster the social strength that binds the family. Meetings create opportunities for social contact, to set shared objectives, foster pride and a sense of belonging. That sense of unity is a source of inspiration and motivation for the family to work diligently and cooperatively toward a collective vision for their future.

On one level, the focus on the social aspect is, in fact, purely social. The family council can serve to foster the continuity of the family as a social entity that, even as its get bigger, more spread out, and more diverse, remains a family that wants to come together. The council's job is to facilitate continuity in the business and the family by providing opportunities for learning, collective development, and fun. One measure of success is that family members don't want to miss a family retreat because they feel that the meetings are productive and serve the family effectively. And, often families attend simply to see other family members who are not part of their everyday lives.

We feel it is important for the family to have fun together—but not just fun for fun's sake. A family council can help establish a rhythm of family members connecting with one another on a regular basis. That's particularly important for members of younger generations—children and teenagers who get to know each other at a young age, if they live in the same town or on opposite coasts. Moreover, by the time those youngsters are adults and have to work together, they're not interacting as second or third cousins whom they're meeting for the first time, but with other people whom they have grown to know and trust. The strength of those relationships plays an integral role in achieving effective and smooth business and family transitions.

Another valuable aspect of the social responsibility of the family council is the managing the details of family get-togethers. In working with families, we recommend that family gatherings be roughly focused in thirds, divided as follows:

- **Fun.** "Fun" is defined and interpreted many ways, but may include activities like group hikes, golf outings, fishing, sitting around the pool, picnics, games, or other forms of enjoyable recreation. Family gatherings should offer enough fun to make them appealing. And activities should be selected so they are inclusive of the interests of the broad group.
- **Education.** This covers a wide spectrum of topics, some of which include education about the business, financial analysis, estate planning, personal and/or professional development, team building, affinity groups, philanthropy, wealth management, and parenting.

- **Development.** It is critical to business and family continuity that the family develops policies together, with the family council taking the lead on ensuring the completion of these initiatives. This might include developing a protocol for elections, family employment, content for future family retreats or education ideas for the next generation.

For larger families, the family council plays an important role in ensuring that the diverse interests of the family are represented. Absent a family council, often the voices of those more active in the business, or family members who are most vocal about their concerns drive the family agenda. As a family grows and increases in diversity in all sorts of ways, a family council can create a climate of inclusion, support and, in particular, safety. While it may be surprising to some, a sense of safety is very much an issue in some families. In working with a number of families, we have repeatedly heard family members comment about how they don't feel safe talking about a particular topic or broaching an issue, especially if some of the other family members have a hostile attitude. A family council can help foster an inclusive climate of safety, so that family members can feel comfortable and secure talking about any issues they feel are important to address.

Specific to the issue of continuity, the council can also help guide the discussion of what precisely the family wishes to perpetuate from one generation to the next. A council can prove the ideal forum for discussing a vision for the family. What is our idealized vision of the future? What among our values, reputation, or legacy do we wish to see maintained? What do we hope to achieve over time?

For instance, many families aspire to be a happy, cohesive group that, over the course of one generation to the next, continues to enjoy working with one another. Through regular meetings and various planned activities and programs (such as educational opportunities around specific topics, a family ski weekend, meeting with another business-owning family, or a family newsletter), a council can work to ensure that those core principles—a bedrock of the family's overall continuity—are maintained and consistently conveyed to all family members.

An active family council can also help delineate decision-making responsibilities and a clear sense of what issues belong to whom. It's common for many families to experience confusion as to which body is empowered to make particular decisions. The council can help educate the family that certain decisions specific to the operation of the business rest with the board of directors. A family member should not pick up the phone and call his second cousin who is the CEO and tell him he thinks they should buy a company that his friend owns in Texas. A family council can help family members understand that such behavior is not only inappropriate, but that those sorts of decisions are handled by either management or the board of directors.

Naturally, there are gray areas, and some decisions require input from both the business board and the council (and perhaps other committees or governing bodies). Families often establish a liaison in the family who is responsible for ensuring that appropriate information is communicated between entities.

Although some of the board's business is understandably confidential, there are decisions that should be shared with and understood by the council. Accordingly, many family councils designate a representative who attends some or all board meetings and reports back to the council. In that way, the council serves as an important communication link between the board, and the family.

Policy Development in the Family Council

The council is typically responsible for developing guidelines or policies for family members, typically after soliciting input from other family members. While this may sound somewhat paternal, there is significant value in policy development. Absent policies, individual decisions may be debated by various family members, and no processes exist to arrive at a decision. Not only is this inefficient but it is unfair; decisions may be perceived as biased, inconsistent with previous decisions made for others, and unpredictable as an approach to deal with family and business issues in the future. Take the case of a policy concerning family employment within the business. A next-generation family member who aspires to a leadership role in the business will have a higher comfort level with a set process that is perceived as objective, predictable, and fair.

Consider the following questions that commonly come up in family businesses:

- How will I know if I'm qualified to take on a leadership role in the business?
- Who will conduct my performance evaluation so I know where I stand and how I might improve?
- What happens if a second-generation sibling believes their child is best suited to take on the CEO role, but others in the family do not feel the same way?
- How can we terminate an incompetent family member with the least amount of damage?
- When can I sit on the business board?
- Why is my cousin paid so much more than I am?

One advantage of developing processes for decision-making that are applicable to all family members is that it proactively mitigates conflict, confusion, and resentment. While family members might resent an ultimate decision that is not in their favor, there can be less ill will if a clear process for that decision was developed and communicated to the family.

The number and formality of policies will depend on several factors, such as the stage of the business, the size of the family, the culture of the family and the business, and overall family harmony[1].

Below is a list of policies and guidelines that families often develop together:

- meeting ground rules,
- family code of conduct,

- family employment policy,
- distribution or dividend policy,
- compensation policy,
- philanthropy policy,
- conflict of interest policy,
- decision-making policy,
- shared property policy,
- media/publicity policy,
- shareholders agreement,
- prenuptial policy, and
- family loan policy.

This list may seem very long to some readers. You might feel that in your family, two or three policies are sufficient for now, and others might be developed over time. Often families decide on which policies to start with based on need. You might have two or three next-generation members coming into the business in the next couple of years. If possible, a family employment policy should be in place before they arrive. Other families choose less contentious policies first, which are typically easier to develop—ground rules, conduct, or philanthropy.

How do family and business policies serve continuity and succession? When family members feel that a level playing field has been created for them, with strong family inclusion and communication throughout the process, they become more engaged. If they perceive that the business operates within a culture of meritocracy and fairness and that expectations and accountability issues have been defined for everyone, they are more likely to commit their allegiance to that environment through future transitions.

Family Council Structure

By definition, the family council represents and reports to the entire family, focusing on a variety of areas. As mentioned earlier, the overall family is often referred to as the family assembly, or at least the family members above a defined age. The size of a family assembly can dictate the size of the family council. For instance, if a family has 38 members, a family council of 5 members might be a suitable size to offer adequate representation without becoming too unwieldy in size. By contrast, if a family only numbers 7, all 7 may also sit on the family council.

The composition and structure of the council typically reflects the size and complexity of the family. As an acid test, it's important to ask yourself if the family council structure is capable of responding to the growing needs of the family. For instance, if you have several branches within the family, it would be great to have participation from qualified, willing participants across at least most of the branches. And, if there are members of multiple generations of a family in the assembly, generational representation is appropriate on the council as well. But don't go overboard. In our experience, six to ten members is generally the recommended size of an effective family council.

Here are a couple of examples to illustrate how family councils can differ. Dave and Stella Perez are brother and sister, and members of the second generation of ownership. Both are married, and both have two adult children. Dave's two children work in the business. Stella's children do not. Dave and Stella have already begun gifting their shares to the next generation as part of their estate planning. The ownership transfer will ultimately result in four equal owners among those four cousins. Accordingly, the Perez family formed a family council to ensure that all third-generation family members would be educated about the business. They also wanted to develop opportunities to make ownership and family decisions together despite the fact that only two family members work in the business.

With Dave and Stella's spouses, the total number of family members at this stage is eight. Given the size of the family and the desire to involve everyone in the business as much as possible, the Perez family decided that all family members would be on the family council. It made sense—with so few members, each family was not only a representative but a constituent as well.

The Wolinski family is much larger. They have 10 third-generation cousins and 37 fourth-generation cousins. With spouses, the family is close to 80 members. In their case, a family council that included every member of the family would be unworkable. Accordingly, the Wolinski family council numbers seven representatives. That is a sufficient size to ensure that members of the family are adequately represented, but not so large that the family council has difficulty functioning effectively.

The Family Council Charter

A family council charter is a document that includes purpose, roles, responsibilities, and high-level goals of the council. In many ways the charter serves as the operating manual for the family council. An effective charter gives clarity to decision-making at the family council level as well as the broader family. It will contain processes for identifying members of the family council, terms and conditions for family council membership, and an overview of the family council's structure

No matter the responsibility that is to be undertaken—be it by a member of the family council or a member in some sort of leadership capacity—it is essential to choose members based on qualifications. Just as a business selects employees based on experience and qualifications, so, too, should a family council be established with those sorts of parameters in focus. To do that effectively, a family council needs to be clear about its purposes and areas of responsibilities. These are described in the family council charter (a sample charter is included in the appendix).

The practice of defining the family council's responsibilities can help in development of criteria desired in council members. While, as we have noted, branch origin can be a factor, don't make the mistake of overlooking other important attributes and qualifications, including

- communication skills—An ability to listen, persuade and inform;
- win-win negotiation and group diplomacy skills;
- maturity;
- understanding and support of the family mission and vision;
- accessibility to the entire family; and
- respect and trust from the entire family.

Some families also establish other parameters regarding membership on the family council. In some instances, families set a minimum age of membership (for example, all members must be at least 25 years old). Additionally, in some cases, family members cannot join the council unless they have previously participated in some kind of leadership role elsewhere, perhaps on a committee or a foundation. Those sorts of guidelines not only establish prior leadership experience but may also encourage prospective family council members to take the responsibility seriously.

An additional issue that can help family councils function more effectively is the inclusion of in-laws on the council. Looked at in one way, if families choose to limit membership to blood relatives, they may well run out of prospective family council candidates, not only in terms of qualifications but also in terms of those family members who are eager to serve.

Including in-laws has been a core component in successful family councils for other reasons. For one thing, given that they have not grown up in the family, they can lend a fresh perspective to certain issues and challenges. They're not hampered by emotional baggage. They can lend diversity and energy. In our experience, we often see in-laws being particularly active participants on family councils because, put broadly, the whole experience is fresh and exciting. That's a valuable commodity to leverage. In addition, they, too, are parents of the next generation of owners.

The family council charter also specifies how often the council will meet. The question of how frequently a family council can meet and function effectively is, like many other issues, particular to the needs of the family. In larger families, quarterly meetings are fairly typical, and meetings often last for one or two days. In smaller families, the council might only meet for a day, two or three times a year.

Face-to-face meetings are generally most effective, particularly when important items are to be considered. In-person meetings can be augmented by conference calls or video-conferencing when necessary.

The Chair and Committees

Once the role of the family council has been defined and members selected, one family member is selected to chair the family council. The chair is typically appointed by the council, but in some cases the entire family must vote for the chair. An effective chair is energetic, takes the entire family into account when performing leadership responsibilities, and always bears the family's vision and overall values in mind. A successful chair acts in the best interests of the overall family without showing bias toward any one particular branch.

Some families may also use the chair position as a method of developing leadership skills among family members. This can be effective, but additional resources such as family advisers or administrative support may need to be leveraged to help organize and implement family initiatives.

Further structure is created within the council through the establishment of committees, charged with overseeing certain areas of various family issues. In many cases they include

- **family events:** a committee that works to organize family retreats and other sorts of regularly scheduled gatherings;
- **communications:** a group that is charged with making certain that all family members are kept informed of the family council's activities and decisions as well as

business matters for which the council takes responsibility to communicate;

- **education:** a committee that works to help educate all family members about various aspects of the business, as well as other topics relevant or of interest to family members, often with a key focus area on the development and education of the next generation (ranging in age from toddlers to college age); and

- **ad-hoc committees:** committees that are often created to focus on a single initiative, such as a family employment committee (to develop policy around that issues), a shared property committee (to develop expectations for shared vacation properties), and an in-law orientation committee (to develop a process of orienting in-laws to the family and the business).

All committees and task forces play a central role in helping ensure smooth continuity in the family. As families grow, a sense of togetherness and unity becomes more difficult to maintain. Through active and effective family events and communications committees, a family council can act proactively to keep the family informed and connected. Further, the education committee plays the important role of making certain that all family members, particularly younger ones, grow in their knowledge and experience as they move toward positions of leadership in the family.

As you can see, family governance is no less important than business governance, for the same and for different reasons. In our experience, families that pursue even some formality around meetings, policy development, and family connectedness dramatically increase the chances of engagement and interest in continuity.

In Brief

- A family council's core focus is on family development and continuity. As a family grows and becomes more complex, a family council can help foster a sense of unity and shared purpose.

- A family council can help foster family continuity through social events, consistent communication with the family, and the development of effective educational programs. Many councils have subcommittees charged overseeing these responsibilities.

- While many families may feel they don't yet need a family council, establishing a decision-making group proactively can help address issues before they grow into significant challenges..

- While it can be prudent to have family council members from various parts of the family, members should also be chosen according to qualifications and experience.

- A family council charter can be very helpful in identifying the council's purpose and specific responsibilities.

7

The Critical Role of Organizational Culture in Continuity

This book presents what we believe to be the critical elements of successful continuity. We encourage families to identify and live by their values, which drive the development of an idealized vision for their future together. We advocate strong business and family governance that will facilitate decision-making as well as provide opportunities for effective communication, education, and a sense of connection with one another. Each of these is a necessary component of continuity planning. Yet by themselves, they are not sufficient to ensure continuity. Without a shared understanding of how you as a family will interact with each other and those around you, continuity is threatened. Values play an important role in defining that, but the *culture* of your family and business is often the driving force for the preservation of your enterprise and the enhancement of human and social capital. In this chapter we will define culture and describe the role that business and family cultures play in supporting continuity.

What Is Organizational Culture?

When you step onto a Southwest Airline flight, you can expect all the staff on the plane to have a great sense of humor. When you shop at Nordstrom's, you come to expect great customer service from everyone in the store. When you order an item from L. L. Bean, you know that the person answering the phone will be knowledgeable and friendly. These organizations have distinct cultures. An organization is a collection of individuals with a shared goal. A business is an organization, as is a sports team, a school, a church, or a family. We often think of culture as it relates to geographies or ethnicities. And certainly we can observe culture based on those visible or articulated distinctions. Organizational culture is more elusive—it's hard to see or even describe sometimes. In fact, we can better understand culture by experiencing it rather than observing it.

Experts in the field of business suggest that culture represents a set of basic values, beliefs, assumptions, expectations, and definitions within an organization. A culture characterizes an organization as well as the participants within that entity. Some people refer to the organization's culture as its "personality" or "the way we do things around here." Some of our clients will describe it as "The (family's name) way." In some family enterprises, the culture of the business is very similar to the culture of the family (particularly when the founder is running the business); in others, distinctions between the two are obvious. The business culture often reflects the values of the founder. Typically, founders are entrepreneurs who have strong ideas about how things should be done and how people should interact. Almost unconsciously, they recruit others who think like they do. This further strengthens the culture. Culture is often so ingrained in the business that, even after the founder's departure, it is perpetuated as a "way of life." This can put your company at either an advantage or a disadvantage. Like any situation, thing, things change. Understanding when to change is crucial to long-term success.

Edgar Schein, who introduced the term "organizational culture," suggests that culture is best understood on three distinct levels. The first level is most visible; this includes things that we see and hear, which are known as artifacts. Some examples include the physical work environment (building design, office layout, furnishings), the way people dress, their style of interaction with each other (be it casual or formal), use of specific language that is unique to the business, company branding, and any other observable behavior. For example, in some office environments, people may address each other by nicknames, while others will be more formal. In some, a closed door may signal a need to knock or even send an email to request a meeting. In others, walking right in is welcome. Some organizations may call a meeting a "huddle" or refer to employees as "team members." All of these are elements of culture that say something about how people work together.[1]

At this level, our understanding of culture emerges from our personal feelings and reactions to what we're seeing. Imagine walking into a physical workspace that is completely open, with no closed or separate offices, where people in the company at all levels share the same space. This might prompt you to describe the culture as highly interactive, non-bureaucratic, and transparent. Yet frankly, the opposite could be true—it is difficult to accurately interpret culture from these surface-level observations. Rituals, ceremonies, and stories within the business represent other observable activities that provide clues to what cultural characteristics exist. For example, you might have an annual awards dinner for accomplished or long-tenured employees, or special athletic competitions that provide opportunities for people to have fun together. Stories or legends, often about the founder, also provide windows of cultural understanding.

The second level of culture relates to what the business espouses or aspires to be, expressed through vision, mission, and values statements, as well as tag lines ("the reliable movers," "the on-time delivery service"). These are assertions made by management. But like artifacts, these may not indicate how members of the organization actually behave. Often they represent more of an aspiration or a way to promote the company to customers, suppliers, or other stakeholders.

Not until espoused values transform into shared beliefs and underlying assumptions—Schein's third level—can we identify the "true" culture of the business or family. At this level, assumptions about people's behavior become embedded and reinforced in the minds of members. Until we recognize these underlying basic assumptions, the interpretations of symbols and espoused values will not uncover the essence of culture.

Think about that for a moment. Do the people in your business or your family actually behave and interact as you espouse to behave and interact? Many businesses claim to be employee or customer focused, espouse that the culture creates opportunities for professional growth, or purport to have a team-based culture. Yet their employees feel neglected, their customers dissatisfied, and the environment is described by insiders as political and competitive. As you can imagine, that has a significant impact on company performance. Families might say they have a communicative, collaborative culture, guided by respect, tolerance, integrity, and other stated values. What we find is that the espoused beliefs and values are not always aligned with the embedded "way" of interacting with others.

The flip side of that misalignment is that family members work so hard at practicing their stated values that it prompts conflict avoidance, which results in missed opportunities for candid, perhaps difficult but possibly game-changing, discussions. As we work with families on generational transition, we often recommend they think about what parts of their legacy they would like to retain and what they would like to leave behind. If families are not willing to consider that their culture needs to evolve, the potentially unattractive outcome speaks to the need for very careful thought when identifying values and expected behaviors as a family. As one example, families that have committed to a culture in which they reward tenure with the business to the point that they retain employees regardless of their fit with the future of the business sometimes need to revisit the impact of this element of their culture and determine whether it is appropriate to retain. After all you don't want the culture to be that all employees know that no matter how they perform they will always have a job.

In this chapter, we will be discussing strong cultures, a term you have likely heard. "Strong" cultures exist when values are consistent with actual behavior, and where all (or most) members share similar assumptions and views of the organization. Strong business cultures impact the selection, training, and retention of employees as well as interactions with other stakeholders. Similarly, families may demonstrate strong cultures as well. One of the reasons that a strong culture can be so powerful is because it fosters commitment from people to a set of values and beliefs that are shared by others. Individuals feel part of something meaningful that is bigger than they are—a collective identity. The impact of culture on continuity is obvious. To the extent that family members feel part of a larger whole, with purpose and meaning, they are more likely to work to promote its continuity.

Why Is Culture Important?

Culture has several characteristics as described above, but two are worth further mention because they both have a significant impact on continuity. The first is that culture cannot be understood by observing overt behavior. Rather, it represents implicit or underlying assumptions and learning that have occurred over years. That means that some (often many) aspects of the culture will be passed onto next-generation family and nonfamily leaders. They will "inherit" culture, which prompts a number of questions from existing leadership:

a) Will our current culture serve the needs of the business and the family, given the changes we anticipate?
b) If not, what initiatives must we take in order to champion cultural evolution?
c) What form must that change take?
d) How will we know if our efforts have been successful?

Passing the baton with a toxic culture is akin to transitioning the business while it suffers from extremely high levels of debt. It is burdensome, and places new leaders at risk for success.

The second characteristic of culture is that it is an embedded abstraction. This makes it "sticky" or challenging to change. Due to its abstract nature, it is often difficult to understand the forces that have created the culture. However, the upside of being sticky is that it makes culture a powerful weapon. But it is an element that you must manage, or else it can manage *you*.

We argue that without awareness of the culture and the variables that influence or create it, leaders cannot effectively serve the evolving needs of the business. The same can be said about culture in the family; family members must understand the elements of culture that facilitate and hinder the family's efforts at continuity. Otherwise, those efforts might be squelched.

Family enterprises are often led and stewarded by family members who are guided by values that were ingrained in day-to-day operations decades earlier and have transcended generations of owners. Those values embody an emotional bond and loyalty from family and nonfamily who are often strongly connected to the legacy of the business. The longevity of those values also helps sustain the uniqueness of the business that supports a distinct culture—perhaps a culture that embodies priorities beyond profitability, such as employees, the community, and the environment. Interestingly, research has shown that companies with a broader focus than profits are more profitable. This was recently confirmed in a 2013 study conducted by Deloitte, titled "Culture of Purpose: A Business Imperative." The study concluded: "What companies do for clients, people, communities and society are all interconnected. A culture of purpose ensures that management and employees alike see each as a reason to go to work every day."[2] This conclusion was also drawn in an earlier study on culture that is specific to family businesses. Family business consultants Denison, Lief and Ward found that family businesses scored higher on all the factors that were used to measure cultural traits:

- adaptability (balancing internal and external events)
- mission (goals and vision for the future)
- consistency (a unified approach to achieving goals and problem-solving)
- involvement (empowerment and teamwork)

In particular, findings showed that family businesses demonstrate stronger congruence, or cultural alignment, and an increased chance of reaching consensus—and doing so more rapidly—on important decisions than do nonfamily businesses.[3]

Hilti, a family-owned business based in Schaan, Liechtenstein, is a manufacturer of tools that are sold worldwide to professionals in the construction, building, and mining industries. Hilti received the Carl Bertelsmann Prize for excellence in corporate culture in 2003, beating out finalists BMW and Novo Nordisk. In his acceptance speech, Pius Baschera, CEO of Hilti, said:

> After hearing the details of our approach to corporate culture, you may have the urge to raise your hand and say "That's your secret to success?!" Our corporate culture is based on the full commitment of top management to a never-ending lifestyle of learning and living the core values of our company on every level for the organization.

Michael Hilti, son of the founder, said that Hilti's culture is likely the most significant driver of success. During his tenure in the business and as chair of the board, he worked hard to communicate and live the values developed by his father and to build a consistently strong culture that permeated the entire organization.[4]

Culture and Your Business

Those who work in the business rely on the culture to guide the way they interact with others both inside and outside the business. When they enter the business, the culture helps new employees learn about ways to interact, and initially increases their comfort level with respect to "how to behave." Because we cannot see and touch culture, we sometimes tend to ignore it when analyzing the success of the business. It's easier to look at the financial statements, or employee skills, or established key performance metrics because we can get our "arms" around those tangible indicators. Those metrics are instructive for leaders in the business and can be used to make important decisions.

We argue that culture is one of the most important indicators of performance for your business primarily because it is pervasive; there is no part of your business that is not impacted by the culture, from design to production to sales to marketing to service. Culture is in all meetings, in offices, and in the halls. It crosses all levels of the business. It impacts those within the organization and those with whom the business interacts. In her book on organizational culture, Marcella Bremer provides a great analogy: "Compare culture to the water in a fish tank that determines whether the fish will thrive or not. The fish are not aware of the water quality but it definitely determines how fast and effectively the fish can swim."[5] Similar to water for fish or air for humans, culture exists and impacts the organization, whether or not we are aware of it. Because culture will exist, regardless of whether you are actively manage it, we advocate it is important to be aware of your culture and the impact it has on performance.

There are a number of determinants of culture; however, we feel the most critical include values, leadership, talent development, and strategy.

Values

The culture of any organization is very much shaped by values. Much of our day-to-day behavior, as well as the decisions we make, is based on the personal values we hold. Some of those values we are consciously aware of, others less so. In a business, culture, by its nature, is based on a collective. A strong culture is dependent on *shared* values. Imagine how those shared values show themselves. They might emerge exactly as you hope, but in the absence of articulated values for which the business stands, people in the business may be guided by their "default" values, which are likely inconsistent throughout the business. Does your accounting department value your customers in the same way the sales people do? Can you say that members of the business consistently model the values that you feel should guide their behavior at work? If the answer is "yes," that's terrific. If your answer is "no," then determining reasons for that is a first step to creating the alignment you seek. Often it is a matter of providing education and communication about the values, and championing those values through strong leadership. When a business articulates a set of values in a written statement, it is often informative to ask employees: "What behaviors or actions do we take that demonstrate these values? What do we do that is inconsistent with these values?"

Ikea is a Swedish, family-owned and operated enterprise in the home furnishings retail space. Broadly known as the world leader for designing, manufacturing, and selling modern and inexpensive functional furniture, first-generation founder, Ingvar Kamprad, originally started out as a "one-man mail" company in 1943. Today the firm counts approximately 70,000 workers and realizes over $33 billion in revenue through 332 stores and 30 franchises spread throughout 38 countries.

Kamprad's personality had a major influence in shaping the company's organizational culture, which was informed by his core values of cost-consciousness, simplicity, and efficiency. His values have also tangibly translated into Ikea's recipe for success: selling good-quality, practical furniture at cheap prices. The multinational founder nourished the company's commitment to cost saving long before he first introduced the "self-assembling" Ikea-way.

Anders Dahlvis, Ikea's CEO from 1999 to 2009, described the firm's culture as informal, cost-consciousness, and with a "down-to-earth approach." It has been famously reported that when IKEA management organized a buffet dinner for employees several years ago, Kamprad served himself last and made sure to shake hands with every worker before they left. Through this genuine and authentic action, the culture of IKEA was further solidified, simply because this humble interaction with employees demonstrated the culture at work in the bones of the organization.

In fact, IKEA's current CEO, Mikael Ohlsson, had this to say about the strong cultural influence of the company's founder: "If we share the same values and the same vision we can put more trust in people working in the organization; we can have a very flat and unbureaucratic organization. We always recruit through values and we spend an enormous effort in strengthening the values: Togetherness, down-to-earth and hardworking."[6]

Leadership

While everyone in the business needs to "own" the culture, it is the responsibility of leaders to create and perpetuate a desired culture. Their job is to model values and ethical standards every day and to make sacrifices for the sake of those values if necessary. Leaders are carefully observed, and their behavior is likely to be mirrored by employees. Respect for leaders emerges from evidence that they "walk the talk." In addition to communicating and living the values, leaders also make the vision for the business real though their every-day behavior. If you are a leader in the business, every statement you make and action seen by employees impacts their perception of you, which in turn shapes the way they interact with each other and stakeholders external to the business.

Talent Development

Naturally, the way in which people are recruited, developed, and managed impacts the development and evolution of organizational culture. Think carefully about your vision for a strong culture. Is it entrepreneurial? Is it a culture that places enough trust in employees so they can make autonomous decisions? Is it a culture that makes employees feel valued, that prompts them to take individual initiative to solve a problem?

Employees thrive in a culture that champions their efforts and that values their ability to self-manage. Nordstrom, another family retailer, has been known for extraordinary customer service since its inception in 1901. Part of the reason for that is because the culture of Nordstrom's has consistently reflected a high level of confidence and trust in Nordstrom employees. For years, new employees were given a 5½ inch by 7½ inch card that represented the employee handbook. It stated the following:

Welcome to Nordstrom

We're glad to have you with our Company. Our number one goal is to provide outstanding customer service. Set both your personal and professional goals high. We have great confidence in your ability to achieve them.

Nordstrom Rules: Rule #1: Use best judgment in all situations. There will be no additional rules.

Please feel free to ask your department manager, store manager, or division general manager any question at any time.

This message is empowering to employees. When they read between the lines above, they might say to themselves, "This company values my judgment," "I have independence," and "They trust me." Despite the fact that the handbook has been expanded somewhat to include some legal regulations and other expectations, the best judgment rule remains the number one policy at Nordstrom's today.

Do your employees get excited about their work? Do they understand the ways in which their efforts make a difference for the business? Do they receive the kind of feedback they need to improve, to inspire them to do better?

We typically see very low turnover in family businesses, which is encouraging. But sometimes the turnover is *too* low. Take a look around at the talent you have and ask yourself whether that talent is serving your values and your vision for the future of the business. Do the members of your business interact in a way that is aligned with the culture you are trying to create? If your answer is "no," you might give some thought to making the necessary changes in order to create the dynamics that drive that culture. You might have experienced this—it only takes one or two people who refuse to contribute to a positive, collaborative, and inclusive environment to infect those around them. A bad attitude, a closed mind, or stubbornness to change can suck the energy out of any effort to maintain a fulfilling experience for others in the business. It can also sabotage the continuity efforts you have worked so hard to ingrain.

In addition to their skills and experience, new employees should be carefully selected for cultural fit. Do they share the same values, might they fit into an environment like yours and contribute to the dynamics of your culture in a way that will strengthen it? In addition, give some thought to how you indoctrinate members into the business. Their experience as a newcomer is important. It is helpful for them to hear the stories, the legend of the business, and to interact with members from all levels of the organization if possible. Everyone plays a role in developing and sustaining a strong culture in your business: management, the board, all employees, and the family.

Strategy

It's likely you have a strategy for your business, whether or not it is stated in writing. Strategy is a plan that is meant to create a competitive advantage for the business, hopefully an advantage that can be sustained over time. It provides direction, articulates goals and objectives, is actionable, and includes various measures for success. We often hear from clients that the growing intensity of competition, industry consolidation, price wars, new competitors, and the effects of technology are among some of the primary sources of competitive rivalry. Margins get squeezed, leading to cost overhauls that still do not make up for reduced profitability. It often prompts management to reevaluate the primary sources of competitive advantage. The culture of your organization might not come to mind first, but research on the culture of family businesses suggests that there is a positive correlation between superior financial performance and superior corporate culture. In order to "win" in your industry today, you have to better and smarter than the next guy. Mistakes are very expensive, with little margin for error.

Another strategic advantage of culture is that it can foster innovation, which some would argue is the primary source of wealth creation. People are responsible for innovation. And the people most likely to innovate successfully are those with the freedom and capacity to develop skills in an organization that has created a learning environment. Toyota is famous for its learning culture as part of its pursuit of product quality and customer satisfaction. "The Toyota Way" includes an emphasis on long-term thinking over short-term financial goals and continuous improvement and learning through every step of the production process. Lean production methods for the last two decades have been led by Toyota, and the unique cultural aspects of The Toyota Way have been virtually impossible to replicate.

Leaders sometimes believe that the strategic plan will drive specific actions and behavior, but that's not true; it's culture that drives behavior. The way people interact with each other internally and with stakeholders externally will determine how effectively your strategic plan is executed.

Organizational culture is a strategic weapon, primarily because it is virtually impossible to imitate. It is so multifaceted and complex that your competitors can look through your windows and try to develop the same culture, but it can never be the same. Culture is like a fingerprint; it simply cannot be copied. A strong culture emerges in family businesses from the permanent "prints" left by the founder but also from the adherence to core principles that have guided the family, often for many generations. Use that weapon wisely by ensuring it is the right weapon for the times. Competitive forces change, and change very quickly in some industries. One cultural characteristic that will help you respond is agility. And creating a culture of agility, in which people embrace change, requires constant awareness and management.

Culture and Your External Stakeholders

Your culture will significantly influence how outside stakeholders perceive and interact with your business. Some of those stakeholders include customers, suppliers, banks, or other financial partners, the community, and possibly the government. While the notion of being "customer focused" seems obvious, not everyone in the business is instinctively tied in to customers' needs or expectations. Reasons for that vary: they may have few interactions with the customers, so it is not a "front-burner" priority; they may have no monetary incentive to focus on the customers' needs; or they may observe other behaviors in the business that suggest the customer is not the biggest priority. How do you as an owner or leader in the business feel when you learn that a customer is unhappy with your product or service? It's hard not to take it personally. Many of our clients suggest that customer service is what truly differentiates their businesses from nonfamily businesses. Therefore a customer-focused culture is a must.

L. L. Bean, a family business based in Freeport, Maine, has won the Customer's Choice Awards several times. CEO Chris McCormick suggests that customer focus is a strong element of L. L. Bean's culture, established more than 100 years ago:

> While today's business environment may differ from what it was in 1912, the philosophy of the company has not changed. Superior customer service has always been and always will be the cornerstone of our brand and is a cultural attribute that differentiates us from the rest of the pack. It originated with L.L.'s "Golden Rule" of treating customers like human beings and our service culture has continued to evolve.[7]

It is not easy to develop, maintain, and strengthen a culture that is focused on multiple stakeholders (stakeholders who change over time and existing stakeholders whose needs evolve). Below is a list of questions you might consider when evaluating how your culture fosters strong relationships with stakeholder groups:

- Do your employees know who all of your stakeholders are and how their actions might influence these stakeholders?
- Do your employees truly understand what you stand for and what expectations you have from relationships with stakeholders?

- Is the style of communication *inside* your business reflective of how it can best serve those on the *outside*?
- Does your culture support efforts to manage stakeholder relationships that provide mutual, rather than one-way benefits?
- Do employees have the opportunity to learn as much as possible about your stakeholders in order to understand their needs?
- Do you provide a variety of ways in which that learning can take place? (Not everyone learns the same way!)
- Do you demonstrate confidence in your employees by giving them the autonomy they might need to best serve stakeholders?
- Has the importance of relationship *longevity* been instilled in your culture? For example, are your employees motivated to seek new customer relationships versus ensuring ongoing customer engagement?
- Have you established metrics of success that reflect what your stakeholders actually think of you rather than your perception of what they think of you?

Building a culture that is focused on long-term continuity means that people on the *inside* need to understand the reciprocity inherent in relationships with people on the *outside*. Research suggests that long-standing relationships with stakeholder groups enhance the value of the business. Companies with a stakeholder focus over a shareholder focus experience higher growth in sales, profitability, and employment growth. In addition, synergies exist across multiple stakeholder groups—you can leverage the trust and loyalty gain from one relationship to serve another.

The Double Edge of a Strong Culture

We've talked about strong cultures and how they serve the family enterprise. When values, beliefs, and assumptions are shared throughout the entire organization, there is an ease and efficiency in how things get done. People are on the same page in terms of what the business stands for and how they go about executing strategy. Strong communication and teamwork create shared learning and effective coordination between departments or divisions. Strong cultures ensure consistency in how employees and stakeholders are treated. In addition, decision-making is expedited when people identify the same priorities and pursue the same desired outcome. Conflict can be resolved more efficiently when core values act as the guiding light in the storm. And ultimately, the culmination of these advantages creates financial success and the preservation of family assets.

Business continuity, is in large part a function of strong culture. In nonfamily businesses leadership changes, together with the absence of (or weak) legacy can create a precarious foundation from which to pursue continuity. Not so in a family businesses, where much of the culture is shaped by the history of the business, the values of the family and a vision that reflects longevity. Continuity is facilitated through generations with the support of a culture that reflects, respects, and is guided by the value created by previous generations.

The flip side of strong cultures is that they can get in the way of meeting your objectives. Imagine a culture that has helped create great success for the business for decades. The values and beliefs that drove behavior resulted in industry leadership. Now, imagine that culture having almost the opposite effect when competing in the same industry today, which looks very different now and requires a different mindset in order for companies to compete successfully. Further imagine detaching people from that embedded behavior. You might have experienced this challenge; it is extremely difficult. Moreover, the consequences of unsuccessful attempts to change represent an enormous threat to business continuity.

J. M. Smucker used to make private label jam for supermarket chains. But third-generation family member Paul Smucker made the risky decision to reduce sales in the short term in order to become a branded-products-only company. Needless to say, this approach has contributed significantly to the continuity of the business through the development of one of the strongest brands in America. A new challenge for fourth-generation members, Tim and Richard, resulted in adding structure and formal process to the business, with new nonfamily, highly skilled managers, formal strategic planning, and new financial concepts. This represented a significant, and surely very difficult, cultural evolution, but one that set the company up for significant growth through the acquisitions of Jif peanut butter, Crisco cooking oil, and Pillsbury baking products, further securing continuity for future generations.

In addition to resistance to change, sometimes subcultures emerge in businesses. This, too, presents challenges when executing strategy. Some businesses have multiple divisions, and often "silos" emerge, each with its own unique culture. While this isn't necessarily a bad thing (in some cases, it is even required), cultural distinctions within the same company create leadership challenges when attempting to align managers' thinking on various strategic decisions, such as expansion, capital allocation, risk management, and talent development. You may run a multibusiness enterprise that requires cultural distinctions, and without these distinctions, some of the businesses would likely be less competitive. What we encourage leaders to pursue in cases in which sub- or "mini" cultures exist is the perpetuation of a dominant, "corporate" culture, under which core values and perceptions of the company's future are shared across multiple entities. The same objective can be said for the extended family, in which subcultures are natural across nuclear families.

Culture and the Family

Just like businesses, every family has its own culture, whether or not it has a family business. Much of what we have presented above regarding the business is analogous to the family system as well. Family and business continuity can be built into the culture of both entities, so that your planning and your actions reflect the needs of the family's future.

What is interesting about culture is that it is based on collective perceptions and behaviors. And working together as a family to create alignment is important (through family meetings or retreats, education about family assets, and strong communication). At the same time, the family culture shouldn't thwart individualism; if family members feel that they are enslaved to behaviors and beliefs that rob them of their uniqueness and distinct thinking, then culture cannot be strong. Many families work hard at managing this paradox, and it can be done!

Continuity is dependent on creating a common understanding across family branches and generations. It also depends on alignment between your *espoused* and your *actual* values, beliefs, and behaviors. Continuity is also dependent on cultural evolution over time. There may be cultural attributes in your family that have "stuck" for generations and that serve as destructive inhibitors to continuity. Your job as a family is to determine what those are and gain a collective understanding of what optimal change looks like.

Does your culture nurture family members in a way that creates commitment and engagement? If it does, that's great, and it must be preserved. No one can understand the unique attributes that serve continuity better than family members, and preservation of those cultural attributes must always remain at the top of your to-do list.

Even Warren Buffett, one of the most successful and well-known business leaders in the world, made a decision to maintain "family" in his business. Buffett decided to preserve "The Berkshire Hathaway Way" when he selected his son Howard, who is a farmer and philanthropist, to succeed him as chair of the Berkshire board. When asked about the rationale for his choice, Buffett suggested that Howard would ensure that the culture of Berkshire is preserved, implying that the preservation of the culture ranks high in perpetuating the business.

The culture of your family is unique, and can provide family members with a sense of pride, strength, comfort, and inclusion. They are part of a collective energy that is experienced, better than described. It's like a recipe—with the right ingredients and the proper care, the outcome tastes very good.

Recipe for a Healthy Family Culture

Number of Servings: Everybody
Please note*: You will have to change the amount of each ingredient and add the "special" ingredients known to your family. Cooking time will vary depending on the temperature of your oven.*

Ingredients

- one set of clearly articulated values
- full alignment of a desired family vision for the future
- several policies and guidelines that provide clarity around expectations and hopes
- strong communication
- respect for diverse opinions and perceptions
- two governing bodies, one for the family and one for the business
- genuine humility
- many bunches of give and take, patience, and support
- loads of love
- buckets of trust

Mix all ingredients together, and adjust amounts as needed for best outcome.

Changing Your Culture

The ability to realize the need for and willingness to embrace change needs to be a core competency in *both* your business and the family if you are pursuing continuity. An explosion of information can characterize most industries. That, combined with globalization and technological quantum leaps, has virtually eliminated stability and made change the norm. A solution to a problem today is exactly that—a solution for the moment, and not one that will necessarily persist as a solution or be applied to future problems. And you will rely on the culture of your organization to respond to the need for change as your business evolves.

We often have requests from clients asking for help to change the culture in their business. While setting an objective for such a change might be the right thing to do, it cannot be accomplished easily or quickly. Imagine trying to change your DNA. Cultural attributes are not impossible to change, but as we mentioned above, they are "sticky."

In their article on cultural change, Katzenbach, Steffen and Kronley, suggest that "you can't trade in your company's culture in as if it were a used car." Culture is what emerges from history, values, ingrained communication styles, and individual and collective behaviors. The authors also suggest that cultural change is best realized by focusing on a few critical shifts in behavior to begin with and honoring the strengths of your existing culture.

There is no magic wand for cultural change, and our advice is to pursue *incremental* versus radical cultural change. Examine what is working and what is getting in the way of continuity for either the business or your family. Below is a brief checklist for you to consider when thinking about cultural change:

- How would we describe our culture now?
- What is great about our culture and what about the culture should we sustain?
- How does our culture help move us toward our goals?
- What behaviors, systems, and policies reinforce a culture we are proud of? How do they provide that reinforcement?
- What about our behaviors, systems, and policies threatens a strong culture?
- What do we need to change, and what would the optimal result look like?
- How should we go about making those changes?

Where is your greatest leverage for cultural change? You can achieve significant change with incremental efforts if you can identify the sources of that leverage. It might be in the energy of one small team, or pockets of ambition that you capitalize on, or leadership resources you have not sufficiently tapped. In our experience, leaders cannot *tell* people to change—they need to BE the change, and they need to engage and empower others to drive change. Without that, the effort is futile. We have plenty of evidence among our clients that suggests targeting appropriate change increments, as well as modeling the behaviors associated with the change will likely lead to your desired outcome.

In Brief

- Culture represents a set of basic values, beliefs, assumptions, expectations, and definitions within an organization.
- Without awareness of the culture and the variables that influence or create it, leaders cannot effectively serve the changing needs of the business.
- It is important to make certain that your organization and family acts according to your culture rather than merely paying lip service to it.
- Four components that help shape culture are values, leadership, talent development, and strategy.
- Culture is not just for insiders. Culture impacts how those outside your business see you.
- It is helpful to examine your business and family culture to determine what about it is effective and what warrants change.
- We advocate that you pursue cultural change incrementally rather than in a more sweeping, radical form.
- Strong cultures serve as a foundation for continuity across business and family transition.

8

The Road Ahead

Based on our years of experience with businesses of all sizes and forms, we feel strongly that well-orchestrated continuity planning is one of the key elements in the success of multigenerational family enterprises.

We consciously included the term "roadmap" in the title of the book for two reasons: first, continuity is a journey, one that has no definitive conclusion; second, maps are tools that guide us to a specific destination. One difference in this case is that the destination on a map is a fixed point; continuity planning is a destination as well as a moving target. By its very nature, it is never complete and will require different roadmaps as the journey unfolds through generations. It is one of the many aspects that make the journey both fun and rewarding.

To reinforce the value we see in comprehensive continuity planning, we conclude with a brief review of key points and bring them together into a unified whole. In Chapter 1, we introduced you to the concept of continuity planning and outlined its many advantages, among them, family consensus and motivation around a shared vision for the future, coordination of critical business and ownership decisions, and the ability to tackle tough family issues in a proactive and productive manner.

Chapter 2 addressed the importance of vision and values in a family's continuity planning process as the foundation that provides the purpose and parameters for the plan. We also drew a clear delineation between the terms "vision" and "values." Vision refers to a long-term outlook: What do you as a family see as the ideal long-range outcome for your business as well as your roles as stewards of the business and legacy to subsequent generations? There are multiple benefits to developing a vision for the family and the business:

- When there is an agreed upon destination, the roads you will travel to get there become more obvious.

- Vision can be used as a yardstick for future debates and decisions.
- A shared vision gives confidence to the elder generation to take a step back and let the next generation assume responsibility.
- The process of setting the vision gives voice to all members of the family across generations and roles, and can build trust throughout the group.

While vision is longer term in nature, values guide your day-to-day behavior. Values are an important component of continuity planning for a number of reasons:

- An articulated statement of values provides family members with a common base of beliefs and expectations.
- Articulating commonly held values educates next-generation family members on the family legacy and expectations.
- Values serve as a rudder in times when everything is going well and provide context for making decisions in tough times when those values might be put to the test.

Vision and values statements should reflect your family's history, the legacy that has been developed over the years, as well as the evolving needs of emerging generations in the family. To be effective in serving as a part of the roadmap for continuity, these statements must be thoughtfully developed, capturing the true nature and expectations of your family. Moreover, these must be inclusive of all family members and engender their commitment. These statements should inspire family members and foster pride, which will ultimately motivate continuity.

The next chapters separated the topics of ownership and leadership continuity, focusing first on ownership. A comprehensive ownership continuity plan addresses not only who will own the business in the future but how and when ownership will be transferred. Like other issues central to the global issue of continuity, we urged family members not to take future ownership as a fait accompli, but rather to work proactively to agree on a suitable ownership continuity plan and execute it thoughtfully.

Due to the financial and legal implications of ownership transition, this area benefits from involvement of external advisers to provide insights on estate, financial, and tax planning. At the same time, these technical issues should not drive the planning process. The family's vision should serve as the foundation of ownership continuity, addressing key questions: How does the family feel about including stepchildren, in-laws, and nonfamily management in ownership? Is ownership a gift, a legacy from prior generations, or something that is earned? Is it important to tie ownership to involvement in the business or should nonemployed owners participate? These and other ownership continuity decisions are guided by a clear vision. As in development of the vision, inclusion of family members is important to the process. There are never circumstances under which ownership transition plans and estate plans should result in surprising family members after you're gone.

In Chapter 4, we laid out strategies for designing and implementing a leadership development and continuity process, starting with a clear definition of your business' leadership needs. Once these needs are defined, the next step in the leadership continuity process is to create a plan to ensure there are future leaders prepared to fill these requirements. We discussed important aspects in preparing future leaders, including the value of first working outside the family business, the critical role of mentors and other guides, and the importance of earning respect and authority. We addressed the importance of viewing leadership development as a process for the entire organization, not just one selected leader. No leader can be successful without a well-trained team to support her. We also emphasized the importance of communication and transparency in the leadership succession process to ensure that family and nonfamily members alike see the process as fair and designed to achieve the best leadership outcome for the business and the family.

Chapter 5 addressed the role of business governance in continuity planning and the importance of ensuring continuity in business governance. The governance structure is responsible for oversight of the business, ensuring accountability of management, and providing input into key decisions. That influence carries over into leadership development, strategic planning, and ownership succession dynamics within the family.

We advocate for an active board of directors to provide this influence and oversight, regardless of business size, age, or profitability. In addition to addressing a variety of continuity issues, board members can serve valuable roles as mentors or confidantes to family members over time. And as we point out, you do not forgo the need for business governance if you feel a board doesn't suit your needs. Business governance is important under all circumstances, and can have a material impact on continuity. Ownership or family groups can also provide oversight to the business and continuity planning process. Just as you need to think about continuity of your leadership group, you need to plan for continuity in business governance. Developing the next generation of board members is critical to the success of the enterprise.

Chapter 6 addressed the role of family governance in continuity planning. Similar to business governance, we advocate that a strong family decision-making structure and process are crucial to continuity regardless of the size or age of the family and business. Whether through informal family meetings or a more structured family council, thoughtful family governance results in prudent decision-making for the family and the business and certainly supports continuity efforts.

With that in mind, we are strong proponents of establishing a family council. A family council can foster family unity and help plan events to build family bonds, as well as provide a forum for education, discussion, and decision-making.

Chapter 7 addressed the importance of organizational culture in helping to ensure continuity. As we discussed, culture emerges from a culmination of many "inputs," some of which include core values, beliefs, expectations, and underlying assumptions. Your culture creates very specific internal behaviors, and will also significantly shape the way outside stakeholders view and understand your business. We encourage you to examine carefully the list of questions presented in Chapter 7 as part of a cultural audit that will help indicate needed changes.

Our brief recap serves as a reminder that continuity planning involves hard work, careful thought, and commitment. Throughout the book, we reinforce a number of factors critical to effective continuity planning.

1. **Vision is the foundation.** Continuity planning should be based upon a clear and thorough family vision that defines the family's aspirations for its future as a business-owning family and guides decisions in all areas of planning.
2. **The process of the plan is as critical as the outcome.** The time spent working through issues increases the quality of the output and develops trust and understanding across all parties involved.
3. **Opt for inclusiveness.** The quality of the outcome as well as its acceptance by the family will be enriched by including family members young and old, employed and not employed, and those with ownership stakes large and small.
4. **Planning should not be rushed.** Development of vision, values, and plans may require multiple iterations and the opportunity for family members to think through the implications of their decisions before they are finalized.
5. **Strong family and business governance enhance the quality of planning.** They provide oversight and accountability to the process.
6. **Planning is an ongoing process.** While plans should be adhered to, they will need to be revisited with incorporation of new generations or changes in business or family environment to ensure their relevance.

The results of solid continuity planning make all that effort remarkably worthwhile for a number of reasons:

- **It is emotionally fulfilling.** Since both the business and your family are dear to your heart, there's no question that everyone involved wants to do the very best they can to ensure that both entities thrive. In this sense, continuity planning melds the affection for business and family into a focused effort—balancing the two to help ensure the greatest benefit for all participants. In many respects, continuity planning is a labor of love.
- **It is economically fulfilling.** Continuity planning not only helps address issues in the here and now, it also adopts a long-term view of making certain that both the proper policies and people are in place for years to come. It serves as a foundation from which strategic direction for the business is developed and executed, which can ultimately create the competitive advantage you need to sustain the business through generations. A successful business is economically rewarding for shareholders as well as other stakeholders associated with the business.
- **It fosters an environment of constructive productivity.** Any successful family business is certainly productive. But continuity planning takes that beyond the realm of business and helps bridge the many issues that are housed in both the family and the business system. By addressing issues such as vision, values, and other topics that focus squarely on what a family values most, family members learn to work together, both within the business itself as well as within the family. And as the family develops meaningful policies together and makes important decisions that support continuity, they develop trust, respect, and a sense of family pride and confidence in their ability to get things done.
- **It provides long-range clarity.** A prosperous family business requires a clear sense of where it is going— and why. Continuity planning helps everyone—family

members and nonfamily members, as well as inactive family shareholders—know and understand the roadmap for the future. Everyone involved can understand where the business and family are going as well as the rationale for that specific direction.

- **Continuity planning brings the family together.** In its own way, this may be the most valuable benefit afforded by continuity planning. As family members work together on long-term issues such as appropriate ownership and leadership, they're also building a sense of unity and togetherness—not merely shared goals and objectives but a shared commitment to achieving them. That creates a powerful bond that permeates both the family as well as the business.

We encourage you as a family and as business leaders to embrace the opportunity of working together on the critical process that is continuity planning. Together, you can craft a roadmap that fits your family and inspires you to work together as stewards of a valuable enterprise. In so doing, your children and their children will be inspired to do the same.

Related Materials

Chapter 5

Sample Board of Directors Charter

The charter and corporate governance guidelines have been adopted to assist the ABC Board and its committees in the exercise of their responsibilities. The board of directors will review this charter annually and, if appropriate, revise this charter from time to time.

Operation of the Board

The responsibility of the directors is to exercise their business judgment to act in what they believe are the best interests of the company and its shareholders. Directors should be entitled to rely on the honesty and integrity of the company's senior executives and its outside advisers and auditors.

In furtherance of its responsibilities, the board of directors is responsible for

- the approval and monitoring of strategic, business, and capital plans of the corporation;
- challenging management thinking and offering new perspectives that will help realize strategic objectives;
- defining performance expectations and holding management accountable to appropriate oversight;
- committee participation;
- providing guidance on leadership and ownership succession;

- perpetuating the values of shareholders and the business;
- assessing risk factors that affect the organization;
- ensuring that the business yields a reasonable return to shareholders.

Board and Committee Meetings

Board meetings will be held four times per year, and special meetings will be called as necessary. A schedule of regular meetings will be provided to the directors well in advance. Directors are expected to attend all meetings, and should spend the time required to properly discharge their responsibilities. Directors should be available to senior management and shareholders as needed. Independent directors may meet in a separate session whenever they feel it is appropriate.

Agenda Items for Board and Committee Meetings

The chair will establish the agenda for each board meeting. At the beginning of the year, the chair will establish a schedule of agenda subjects to be discussed during the year (to the degree this can be foreseen). Each director is free to offer suggestions to the chair for agenda topics. A detailed agenda and any related documents will be provided to all directors approximately ten days in advance of each board meeting.

Director Compensation

Independent directors will be paid quarterly. Shareholders will not be compensated for their position as director.

Director Orientation and Education

Management will provide new directors with an initial orientation to enhance their understanding of the company. Each director with receive a Board Resource Book that will provide various documents, some of which include:

- articles of incorporation
- a strategic plan
- a board charter
- directors and officer insurance
- bios of each director as well as key senior executives
- the ownership structure
- an organization chart
- financial statements for the last three years

Board Structure

Board size will range in number from seven to nine people. The board is responsible for nominating members to the board and filling vacancies that may occur.

The board will review on an annual basis its own performance and discuss the requisite skills and characteristics of new board members as well as the composition of the board as a whole. Analysis of board composition will consider diversity in terms of age, skills, and experience.

Any director may resign at any time by giving notice in writing or by electronic submission to the chair of the board. The resignation date will be determined with the chair and other board members.

Directors will ensure that the board is notified of any and all other directorships with both for-profit and not-for-profit organizations. Any discussions that take place at the board will be considered confidential. Directors are expected to sign a confidentiality agreement before they begin serving their term.

The standard term of service is three years, subject to annual approval by the shareholders.

Voting

A minimum of two-thirds of the shareholder group will select directors through a voting process. Decisions at the board that require votes will be made with simple majority.

Chapter 6

Sample Family Council Charter

Family Council Purpose

As the representative body of the Family Assembly, the family council is charged with making key decisions on behalf of the family. This might include developing policies, and making philanthropic and educational development decisions. In addition, the family council will create opportunities for family members to remain informed about family and the business, and to connect with other family members.

Family Council Goals

- promote continuity of the family values and vision,
- educate family members, and build understanding of the family enterprises,
- organize communication from the business to the family and from the family to the business,
- plan family activities and organize family meetings,
- create cohesive family group, have fun together, and build strong family relationships, and
- develop and regularly review family-related policies.

Family Council Guiding Principles

- There will be equal opportunity for all family members age 21 and over to participate. Family members are direct descendants of the Rubin family and their spouses.
- The council will seek diverse involvement across generations, including in-laws.
- Focus is on efficiency – using a smaller group to get things done. Education and communication will take place with the entire family in larger meetings, not in family council meetings.

- The process is open and transparent.
- Minutes will be sent to the entire family.

Family Council Meetings

The family council will meet quarterly. The family assembly will meet twice per year, once in the fall and once in the late spring.

Family Council Structure

The family council will consist of eight members, representing multiple branches, generations, and genders. In-laws are encouraged to participate on the family council.

The council will consist of three standing committees: education committee, communication committee, and event planning committee. The family council chair will oversee committee work and hold committee chairs accountable. The family council chair will create meeting agendas and lead all meetings. The family council secretary will take meeting minutes.

Elections and Terms of Service

The family assembly will elect family members to the family council after the nominating committee submits a slate.

Family members will serve a three-year term on the council, with staggered terms. Each family council member may serve a maximum of two terms.

Decision-making

Decisions will be made by consensus; however, when necessary, a majority vote will rule.

Sample Family Meeting Ground Rules

- Everyone brings wisdom.
- All participants are responsible for good ideas.

- Participants are open to listening to new ideas.
- We question what we've always done.
- Everyone has equal status.
- We wear the family hat for these meetings.
- We leave personal agendas and egos at the door.
- We respectfully disagree.
- No one gets picked on.
- No information that we discuss in these meetings leaves the room without approval of the group.

Sample Family Council Meeting Agenda

Meeting Agenda

Saturday, October 2, 2013
9:00 a.m. – 3:00 p.m.
8:00   Breakfast available until 9:00 a.m.
9:00   Catch up

- Please take a few minutes to catch family members up on what is new with you and your nuclear family
  9:15   Family Council Charter
- Review/discussion and ratification of family council charter
  10:15   Break
  10:30   Family Values
- Prioritize the list of values developed by the family assembly members
- Establish a committee to develop a statement of values
  11:30   Family Retreat
- Review of possible locations for 2014 family retreat
  12:00   Lunch
  12:45   Family Retreat Content
- Identify possible content choices for meetings during 2013 family retreat
- Prioritize
- Confirm action items for Planning Committee
  2:00   Committee updates (please read submitted reports in advance of the meeting

- Communication Committee
- Education Committee
- Family Employment Committee
  2:50   Meeting debrief
  3:00   Meeting adjourned

One Family's Journey

Rarely does a family set out with the intention to build a comprehensive continuity plan incorporating all of the elements outlined in the previous chapters. Most commonly, the process starts with a need in a specific area. Such was the case for the Timmons/Pelham family. In fall 2006, 14 third-generation owners of Canal Insurance, Central Realty, and several other smaller entities held their first official family meeting. Their pressing need was to discuss second-generation estate planning, an ownership continuity issue.

"As a group, we became aware that we were dealing with issues we were not comfortable with, such as lack of shareholder representation, generational issues and the focus of ownership authority. There were differing perspectives, which could have had a detrimental effect on family interactions," says Dru James, who served as family council chair from 2008 to 2013. "There were family employment and management issues that no one was comfortable confronting without objective input. There was also a desire for owners to have a collective voice and for the council to provide the organizational structure for this collective voice."

These concerns drove the family to meet again, in the spring of the following year, April 2007. The majority of the group lived within a couple hours' drive of the Greenville, South Carolina, headquarters and several had worked or were working in the business. Despite these close connections and the fact that their ages ranged from late 40s to late 50s, they had not yet developed a process for working together as owners. The intimacy of three second-generation owners with close ties to the companies would be challenged with the transition to 14 third-generation owners, many with little or no knowledge of the companies. This challenge would further increase as the 50-plus fourth-generation members, many living outside of the home office region, began their development as active shareholders. What they did know was that the process that had worked for their three second-generation predecessors would not work for them. And, they wanted to build a system with more information sharing than in the prior generation. Attendance at a family business governance program at the Kellogg School of Management further spurred their interest.

So, at their 2007 retreat, the group decided to engage a consultant to help them determine how to organize decision-making in the third generation. A representative of each of the three family branches was selected to serve as a committee to identify and screen family business consultants. After a search, which included five well-respected family business consultants, Craig Aronoff, one of the founders of the Family Business Consulting Group, was selected to work with the family.

"It helped us to have a 'master of ceremonies' or 'conductor' leading us through topics new to us," says James. "The second generation communicated little about the business, and we became aware as the third generation that we had assets that we wanted to be more informed about and involved with – to be active shareholders."

Aronoff conducted interviews with all 14 third-generation members and presented his findings in a report, *Organizing the Third Generation: Family and Ownership,* which was distributed to the family members in fall 2007. The group held a retreat in Asheville, North Carolina, to discuss the report and identify priorities for determining third-generation decision-making. Central to these priorities was a desire to formalize business and family governance processes. At that point, the insurance business was overseen by a family board consisting of one representative of each of three family branches, two of whom were senior executives in the business. Real estate and investment entities were overseen by more informal boards comprised of owners. What was less clear was who had oversight authority. Additionally, formal meetings were infrequent. The group agreed that adding independent directors on the board of the insurance business, the largest of the three, would be a suitable starting point in formalizing business governance. (As agreed in original discussions, they later recruited independent directors for the real estate company board as well.) "The majority of family members agreed we needed objective and expert guidance for success of the company as a family business. We saw a need for company management and governance issues to be addressed under a more formal and sustainable business structure," says James. "We also saw the need to evolve from a niche company and to have outside directors with experience in insurance as well as evolution of family businesses was necessary."

The group also agreed to create a family organization with a mandate "to hold the family together and sustain commitment to the business, enable family members to get to know each other and build relationships, promote understanding of the business and the family's legacy, train family to be effective owners, and facilitate family decision-making." The 14 third-generation members realized that they had a unique opportunity to provide the fourth and the future generations well-structured and sustainable businesses. This opportunity would become more difficult, if not impossible, if left to the 50-plus fourth-generation members.

Three task forces were formed to execute these priorities:

- the Corporate Governance Task Force, charged with leading the search for the outside directors
- the Family Business Policy Task Force, charged with presenting basic policy recommendations
- the Family Governance Task Force, charged with presenting a draft Family Council Charter

Family members volunteered to participate in the task forces, helping to move the process forward and ensure family buy-in on the recommendations. With a strong family commitment to these priorities, the group settled into a routine of holding retreats twice a year, once in the spring in conjunction with the shareholder meeting and once in the fall to review task force recommendations and make decisions. With the family's dedication to working together between meetings, including speaking with other families about governance structures, reading books on family business, and hashing out options as a group, the task forces were able to propose several recommendations in April 2008.

While the family members undertook a lot of hard work, they also used their meetings as an opportunity to have fun together. Because they had all grown up in Greenville and many of their spouses had grown up with the family as well, they had camaraderie to build upon. The group also took advantage of common interests in college football and shag dancing (a regional dance in the Carolinas) to enjoy some down time between intense family decision-making sessions. One consultant who worked with the group commented, "It was easy to see their joy in being together. After dinner at the first meeting I attended, someone pulled out a CD player and cranked up dance music for the group. Cousins were dancing with each other and their spouses. You could tell they had a great base of family togetherness to build upon."

Working together as a family presented challenges as well as an opportunity to build upon existing family bonds. One of the first challenges was how to make decisions. The group decided that each of the 14 cousins would have a vote and that all recommendations would be approved through a formal voting process and captured in meeting minutes. While the choice of one person, one vote may sound obvious, it created a challenge in balancing the power across family branches. Two family branches had three members each, and one had eight. So, there was concern that the larger branch could dominate decision-making. The group overcame this issue by agreeing on an ability to trigger a branch caucus should the vote by hand seem partial because of the uneven branch sizes.

With the decision on the method for voting to approve decisions under their belts, the group went on to tackle business and family governance structures. At a prior meeting, the group had voiced strong support for independent directors. Between meetings, the task force was able to screen and propose a strong slate of independent director candidates with deep experience in the insurance industry, family business transitions, and corporate governance. In addition to approving outside directors, the owners elected to maintain the three family board representatives. Key to the board selection was identifying directors who fit well with the family and business culture. Directors interviewed with existing family directors as well as with the search committee to ensure they were a good fit.

The time spent identifying strong board members was worthwhile. The board proved to be a critical element of the continuity planning process moving forward, addressing issues including leadership succession in the businesses and development of liquidity mechanisms for shareholders. The board selection task force also provided an opportunity for willing family members to become a part of the process. This education proved valuable in achieving future family council goals.

On the family governance front, a family council structure was approved and initial policies presented for consideration. The group agreed that all 14 cousins would serve as the family council and that a three-member steering committee, with representation from each branch, would be responsible for guiding its activities. A secret ballot vote was conducted with each of the 14 selecting a member from the three branches for the steering committee. The group made the decision that it was important for all members to vote for each branch representative, rather than having the branches choose among themselves. The steering committee then selected a chair.

With a significant amount of work still to be accomplished, the group decided to create several committees of the family council – including a policy and governance committee, a communications and finance committee, and a fourth-generation committee (later renamed the family education and integration committee) to evaluate when and how to incorporate the growing fourth generation. Chairs were selected for each committee.

"It's really all been a work in progress driven by achieving specific goals," says James. "For instance, the Policy and Governance Committee is working on qualifications and development of family directors on the company boards and has been in conversations with the board members. There are also conversations about liquidity opportunities."

While the group was strongly committed to these efforts, they acknowledged the challenge inherent in saddling 14 members with so much work. Feeling this pressure, coupled with the desire to leverage the talents and commitment of many capable spouses, they decided to evaluate the idea of including spouses in the decision-making process by discussing the pros and cons of such a decision.

In September 2008, when the group met again, they agreed to incorporate spouses into their family council, giving each of the 14 family units one vote. The decision of voting units by family was driven by a desire to respect the needs of members who did not have spouses, who would be disadvantaged in a situation where spouses had their own vote.

The expanded council then spent time discussing the family's mission, supported by a draft presented by the policy and governance committee. This mission served as a foundation for defining the family's purpose in working together and as a guidepost for its work going forward.

Our mission is to build on existing family traditions and foster development of new ones, and to make ownership rewarding and meaningful for all shareholders. We will accomplish this as we promote learning, encourage personal well-being, sustain and expand our relationships with one another, build value in our shared business operations, preserve and celebrate our family history, and work to create a better tomorrow for our families and communities, and for the world.

At this meeting, the group also approved a family employment policy to govern inclusion of the fourth generation in the business and a reimbursement policy to determine what expenses related to family council meetings and work would be supported by the business. Decisions on rules for involving fourth-generation members in the business were particularly challenging because there had been no precedent for defined rules when third-generation members entered the business.

The benefits from this dedicated work have been evident. One of the hallmarks of the family's decision-making process has been careful evaluation of all decisions before a final agreement is reached. Topics are typically raised in one meeting, and assigned to a committee or task force to study, with recommendations from the smaller group evaluated at a subsequent meeting. Often, a policy or decision will be worked on by a committee, presented in draft form at one meeting and revisited at the next for final approval. While it takes time, this process ensures that the family carefully thinks through its decisions and their implications.

With the eldest members of the fourth generation about to enter their 40s, and a desire to be more open and inclusive with the next generation than their parents had been with them, third-generation members decided that understanding the perspective of their children was important. Therefore, they engaged consultants to interview next-generation members about their interests and concerns. One of the most crucial questions asked, from a perspective of continuity planning, was whether or not the fourth generation had an interest in being involved as owners in the family's businesses. Through this effort, the response of one fourth-generation member summed up the general sentiment of the group, "Growing up, it was a source of family pride – great granddad started it and it has done so well. I still feel proud that it has done well – so I like that kind of family connection around the business."

Another milestone for the family was naming the family council. After considering several options, the group decided on a name with dual meanings – and the EVA Council was christened. Eva was the name of their grandmother and it also represented the business acronym for economic value added. The group hoped to add value to their assets and their relationships through their work together.

In April 2009, already into their third year of meetings, the group developed a code of conduct governing how they would treat each other, agreed to incorporate independent directors onto the real estate company board, and approved the family education and integration committee's (formerly the fourth-generation committee) recommendation to develop an education program for fourth-generation family members.

When the group reconvened in fall 2009, they elected the real estate entity board, finalized family policies recommended at earlier meetings, and performed an exercise to clarify ownership vision. This important project was undertaken to clarify owners' desires and expectations for the boards as well as create consensus across the ownership group. Topics addressed included financial expectations of the business as well as the role the family desired to play in leadership of their businesses. As can be seen from the excerpt below, the vision statement demonstrates a focus on continuity and provides guidance on many aspects of continuity planning.

The EVA Council vision for our jointly owned entities:

- *We expect our jointly owned businesses to strive for excellence, follow best practices, demonstrate ethical standards, and be market leaders, good corporate citizens and responsible employers.*
- *We prefer family ownership of all business entities as long as family ownership is the best business decision, allowing for exit of those owners who are not interested in maintaining ownership, as feasible in the given business environment.*
- *We believe that entities should be overseen by strong boards of directors incorporating well-qualified independent directors and family directors.*
- *We support oversight of the family by a strong Family Assembly and Council, which provides opportunities for participation to all family members and spouses who*

meet defined criteria. The Family Council serves as the family decision-making body. Voting on family issues is by third-generation family units. Shareholder issues are voted by ownership percentages.

The group reconvened in May 2010 for their annual shareholders' meetings as well as the council meeting. In order to promote family communication and create a way to archive important documents, the council improved an investment in development of a family website, which would also be a place to share family photos and stories and collect council documents.

Another important decision at that meeting was to capture all the EVA council documents, including by-laws, committee charters, vision statement, policies, communication matrices, and EVA Assembly history in the form of a timeline. This document would be called *The EVA Book.*

Thanks to work by the steering committee in-between meetings, the council was able to approve a revised draft of the family vision statement. And, the council ensured its own continuity by electing steering committee members for the third time.

The September 2010 meeting was a momentous one, as it was the first to incorporate attendance of fourth-generation members, an event that had been planned for since the initial creation of the fourth-generation committee two years earlier. Fourth-generation members participated as part of a family assembly, with third-generation members taking part in the meeting for a third-generation-only EVA Council meeting.

In May 2011, with the process for involvement of the fourth generation underway, the question turned to how to incorporate them further into decision-making. The policy and governance committee was tasked with evaluating the existing structure to determine what changes should be made. In fall 2011, the Council approved inclusion of fourth-generation members eligible for membership by policy (21 years of age and completion of an orientation course) to join the current governing body, the EVA Council, and to participate in votes through the existing structure of 14 votes. The policy and governance committee was directed to continue discussions on the next steps in transitioning to a new governance structure and recommend bylaw changes that incorporate the decisions.

In fall 2012, the Timmons family took the final step in creating continuity to the fourth generation by changing their voting structure to allow each family member a vote, dissolving the 14-unit family structure. The group also opened up leadership positions to fourth-generation members and changed the structure of the steering committee to allow for a larger group of participants. By this time, fourth-generation members had already started to make their mark on the EVA Assembly. Through their interest in pursuing joint philanthropy, a philanthropy committee was established, and fourth-generation members planned a group service project.

"The majority of the G4s are in their late 20s and 30s. This is in comparison to G3 initial involvement in family council as a group with the average age in our 50s, so the G4s have more of an opportunity to build on our initial work of putting governance structures, shared vision, and purpose in place," says James. "This is exciting to me, and presents an opportunity for them to provide the definition of what a mature EVA council will look like! They will play an integral role in educating and preparing their generation and the next generation for roles as family leaders and stewards."

Continuity was ensured in spring 2013 when three fourth-generation members joined that leadership group. The EVA Council closed this chapter of its journey by conducting an assessment of the council's strengths and weaknesses, opportunities, and challenges to determine what the next part of their journey should look like. Some of the most important feedback from that exercise included:

Opportunities

- *Use meetings to enhance educational opportunities for EVA as a group, on Canal and family business in general (e.g., how to become better owners)*

- *Clarify EVA mission, vision, and goals going forward, now that initial goals have been accomplished*

Challenges

- *Leadership succession in Council, as G3s are getting older*
- *Next-generation group with skills and commitment required to sit on business boards*
- *Potential for waning participation due to competing demands on time and energy of participants*

This feedback was taken to heart in the planning of the fall 2013 retreat. Up to that point, all family meetings had been held at the beach or in the mountains, within driving distance for most family members. Family members appreciated both destinations as locations of shared family trips in their youth. For the 2013 retreat, the group decided to break with tradition and meet in Chicago. With a meeting focus on education, as identified in the opportunities and challenges exercise, Chicago was chosen due to the proximity of family business education resources at local universities and family business speakers. This move demonstrates the ability to balance tradition with change, an important lesson for families navigating the challenges of continuity planning.

Through hard work, family commitment, and a willingness to tackle challenging issues, the Timmons family has cemented continuity between third- and fourth-generation ownership. No doubt they will continue to have hurdles to overcome. As seen from the exercise above, the current agenda includes considering how to prepare a next generation of family directors and how to maintain attendance at family meetings and involvement in the council in a generation of family members who are more geographically dispersed and face time constraints from young families and jobs.

We are confident they will tackle these challenges with the same diligence and persistence demonstrated through their initial journey. We wish them success on the path ahead.

And, we appreciate their willingness to share their example with other families. Their roadmap will be different than yours, but we hope the diligence and thoughtfulness they have demonstrated in tackling tough issues, their commitment to all aspects of continuity planning, and their ability to appreciate the joy of family will serve as an inspiration.

"In a relatively short time we have gone from 14 G3 members, added spouses, and now have added G4s and spouses for a total of 61 assembly members. We also have 11 G5s under the age of 10," says James. "We are committed to this transition, but are acutely aware of the consequences of disenfranchising any one branch or family. We need to encourage a structure that unites the family and helps members develop competencies. A particular challenge is involving all members in some capacity. Only by working together can we find shared energy and passions and that glue that keeps us together."

Notes

2 The Foundation of Continuity: A Vision for the Future

1. John L. Ward (2004). "The Murugappa Group: Centruies-Old Business Heritage and Tradition," Kellogg School of Management, Northwestern University.
2. John L. Ward, Sachin Waikar, and Carol Zsolnay (2009). "Technical Note: Why Bond? The Benefits of Family Ties across Time, Space, and Generations," Kellogg School of Management, Northwestern University.
3. Credit Suisse Research Institute and Ernst & Young (2011). "Family Businesses: Sustaining Performance." http://www.credit-suisse.com/ch/en/news-and-expertise/news/economy/global-trends.article.html/article/pwp/news-and-expertise/2012/09/en/family-businesses-prove-resilient.html
4. James Hughes Jr. (2007). *Family: The Compact Among Generations*, New York: Bloomberg.
5. Craig E. Aronoff and John L. Ward (2001). *Family Business Values*, New York: Palgrave Macmillan.

3 Ownership Continuity

1. Internal Revenue Service (2009). "Discount for Lack of Marketability." www.irs.gov/pub/irs-utl/dlom

4 Leadership Continuity

1. Amy M. Schuman (2010). *Nurturing the Talent to Nurture the Legacy*, New York: Palgrave Macmillan.

2. Craig Aronoff, Stephen McClure and John L. Ward (2010). *Family Business Succession*, New York: Palgrave Macmillan.
3. Case: Keystone (A), 2005. Prepared by Research Associate Sue Perricelli, Carol Zsolnay, and Professor John Ward, Kellogg Center for Family Enterprises.

6 The Role of Family Governance in Continuity Planning

1. Craig E. Aronoff, Joseph H. Astrachan, and John L. Ward (1998). *Developing Family Business Policies*, New York: Palgrave Macmillan.

7 The Critical Role of Organizational Culture in Continuity

1. Schein, Edgar H. (2010). *Organizational Culture and Leadership*. San Francisco: Jossey-Bass.
2. Deloitte (2013). "Culture of Purpose: A Business Imperative. Deloitte Development LLC."
3. Denison, D., Lief, C. Ward, J. L. (2004). "Culture in Family-Owned Enterprises: Recognizing and Leveraging Unique Strengths." *Family Business Review, 17*(1), 61–69.
4. Lief, C. (2005). *Hilti: Our Culture Journey*. Lausanne, Switzerland: IMD.
5. Bremer, M. (2012). *Organizational Cultural Change*. Zwolle, The Netherlands: Kikker Groep.
6. Ohlsson, Mikael (2013). "IKEA CEO Defends Secretive Culture." *Financial Times*.
7. http://blog.nrf.com/2010/09/14/l-l-bean-president-shares-secrets-to-top-notch-customer-service/

Index

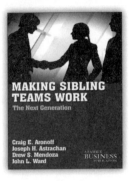

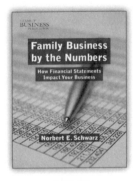